Saying Yes and Saying No

Books by Robert McAfee Brown
Published by The Westminster Press

Saying Yes and Saying No:
  On Rendering to God and Caesar

Unexpected News:
  Reading the Bible with Third World Eyes

Making Peace in the Global Village

Theology in a New Key:
  Responding to Liberation Themes

Is Faith Obsolete?

Religion and Violence:
  A Primer for White Americans

The Pseudonyms of God

The Collect'd Writings of St. Hereticus

The Hereticus Papers
  (Vol. II of The Collect'd Writings of St. Hereticus)

The Significance of the Church
  (Layman's Theological Library)

The Bible Speaks to You

P. T. Forsyth:
  Prophet for Today

Saying Yes and Saying No
On Rendering to God and Caesar

Robert McAfee Brown

The Westminster Press
Philadelphia

First edition

Published by The Westminster Press®
Philadelphia, Pennsylvania

PRINTED IN THE UNITED STATES OF AMERICA

9   8   7   6   5   4   3

Library of Congress Cataloging-in-Publication Data

Brown, Robert McAfee, 1920–
  Saying yes and saying no.

  1. Church and state. 2. Government, Resistance to—Religious aspects—Christianity. 3. World politics—20th century. I. Title.
BV630.2.B76 1986   261.7   85-29575
ISBN 0-664-24695-8 (pbk.)

Contents

To Sydney
who finally said
YES

Acknowledgments

Although some of this material has appeared in print before, most of it has been radically recast. The chapter on Barmen was originally given as a Christian Century Lecture in Seattle, and as the annual Graduate Theological Union Faculty Lecture in Berkeley, before being published in *The Christian Century* and *Seventh Angel*, and the material in chapter 10 has also appeared in *The Christian Century*. The material on Abraham Heschel and prophetic ethics in chapter 3 is adapted and condensed from my chapter in John Merkle, ed., *Abraham Joshua Heschel: Exploring His Life and Thought* (Copyright © 1985 by Macmillan Publishing Company). Part of the material on the Puebla conference in chapter 4 was originally contained in a longer essay in John Eagleson and Philip J. Scharper, eds., *Puebla and Beyond* (Orbis Books, 1979). The material on Alan Paton in chapter 7 is the substance of an article that originally appeared in *Christianity and Crisis*, and the material on anti-Semitism in Poland in chapter 8 is reprinted, close to its original form, from *A.D. Magazine*. Although the material on Grenada in chapter 5 has not previously appeared in English, an earlier version appeared in German in the *Deutsches Allgemeines Sonntagsblatt*, as "Licht vom anderen Amerika," shortly after the invasion.

The rest of the material—the introduction, chapters 2, 6, 9, and the conclusion—has not previously appeared in print and, with the exception of the conclusion, were written expressly for this volume. Fugitive paragraphs from unpublished speeches have also made their way into these pages.

I am grateful to the publishers cited above for permission to adapt earlier words to a fresh occasion and to my daughter-in-law, Karen Friedland, for typing help at the eleventh hour.

I tremble for my country when I reflect that God is just.
> —Thomas Jefferson

I should like to love my country and still love justice.
> —Albert Camus

To listen to a story . . . is to play a part in it, to take sides, *to say yes or no*, to move one way or the other.
> —Elie Wiesel

Those who ignore history are doomed to repeat it.
> —George Santayana

My conscience I have from God and cannot give to Caesar.
> —John Milton

Personal Introduction:
On Rendering to Presbytery

In the years when I used to instruct Presbyterian seminarians in the fine art of preparing for ordination examinations (formal title: Systematic Theology 261: Theology of Presbyterianism, Fridays 2–4 P.M., 2 credits—informal title: How to Get Ordained Though Honest), I used to pass along two pieces of prudential wisdom. (1) As far as you can do so in good conscience, use the Presbyterian buzz words (justification, providence, scripture, authority, johncalvin). (2) Tell the presbyters what you believe rather than what you don't believe.

I still think the advice is good, although no longer as necessary as in those happily bygone days when our sole confessional standard was the 1647 Westminster Confession of Faith—of all the seventeenth-century Reformed confessions the most "scholastic" of the lot, a fact the denomination recognized in 1967 when it added to our doctrinal standards more resilient statements such as the Second Helvetic Confession, the Scots Confession, and the Barmen Declaration of the German Confessing Church.

Forty years after my own ordination, when I faced doctrinal reexamination as a result of transferring my presbytery membership, I decided to forgo both bits of prudential wisdom and use the occasion as a kind of reality check: I would tell the members of presbytery exactly what I believed (to the extent that one can be exact about mystery), in my own vocabulary rather than theirs, and I would also tell them what I did not believe. I would say Yes where I could, and No where I must. Although I was not lusting for failure, I realized that if I was turned down, I could probably survive the rebuff and gracefully "revert to lay status" (as we put it), whereas if I was reaffirmed, I could both rejoice that I made it without fudging and even grease the skids a bit for subsequent ordinands who were restive about playing coy theological games with their elders.

As I worked on a format, the interrelatedness of saying Yes and saying No became increasingly apparent. I recalled that Christians in Nazi Germany, writing the Barmen Declaration (which we will examine in chapter 1), found that they not only had to make their *affirmations* with clarity, they had to spell out the *negations* implicit in their affirmations with equal clarity. The bottom line of this process, I suppose, is the proposition that to say Yes to God means to say No to Satan, since there is no way to say Yes to both. Once the bottom line has been reached, however, there still remains the considerable exercise of deciding which areas of our life manifest God and which Satan, so that we know to whom and to what to say Yes and No, and the rest of this book is devoted to exploring some of the intricacies of that exercise.

I include my presbytery statement here, not only because Part Two is an illustrative exercise in saying Yes and saying No but also because the two parts together will indicate to readers where their author is coming from and allow them to make whatever adjustments in their estimate of these pages may be necessary as a result.

Part One

I believe that the ultimate disposition of who I am is in the hands of One whose hands are ultimately sustaining and gracious, however sternly they have to deal along the way with such recalcitrant cargo as myself.

I believe that I get clues enough and to spare about the nature of reality from ongoing confrontation with the Jesus story and even from occasional confrontation (usually through another person) with Jesus himself.

I believe that such clues are confirmed a hundred-fold by who my wife is, who my children are, and who a few incredibly dear friends continue to be.

I believe that I am part of a further circle beyond those just named, who occasionally manage to put others ahead of themselves and God ahead of all, a circle to which I give the name of "church."

I believe that there are tasks to do that give meaning to our lives, and that the degree of our own individual success or failure is of little consequence, since God empowers others to pick up and fulfill whatever we do for good and to transform and redeem whatever we do for ill.

I believe that conversion is not only about changing individual hearts but also about changing social structures, not just cosmetically but radically. This means chipping away at, and perhaps destroying, many things we have taken for granted, and building into our own situation what many Third World friends have found to be true in theirs, that "to know God is to do justice."

I believe there are little moments when vast things happen: when bread and wine are shared in certain ways; when brisk walks in the woods are shared with certain persons; when someone else says "thank you" to me, or when I remember to say "thank you" to someone else; when children rise up and bless us simply by who they are; when Beethoven string quartets pierce us with both the joy and the woe of our being, the same joy and woe that William Blake assured us are "woven fine, a clothing for the soul divine."

I believe that our lives provide the occasion for flashes of fulfillment, no matter how much they are threatened by surrounding darkness, and that we can even begin by grace to deal with the surrounding darkness, because we have it on high authority that light shines in the darkness and the darkness has not overcome it.

Part Two

Here I follow the form of the Barmen Declaration, linking affirmations with negations. Although the gospel is finally Yes and not No, a No can make explicit what is only implicit in the Yes.

1. *Scripture:* I say Yes to Scripture as our means of access to the story of God's people; I say No to Scripture as a repository of doctrine.

I say Yes to Scripture as radically "good news to the poor," which can also be good news to the rest of us; I say No to Scripture as consolation apart from its radical social challenge.

2. *Jesus Christ:* I say Yes to Jesus, a Jew from Nazareth, who embodies the present reality of God's Kingdom as *Christos* (God's anointed one); I say No to a deified Jesus whose humanity is thereby negated.

I say Yes to Jesus' life, death, and resurrection not only as sources for our own individual transformation but as points of decisive confrontation between the power of God and the power of human society, which tried to destroy Jesus on the cross. God reversed all expectations by the resurrection, and Jesus' followers became citizens of a totally new order. I say No to interpretations of Jesus that reduce these events to an individualistic meaning.

I say Yes to Jesus as the Jew whose mission to the Gentiles makes possible our inclusion in the promises of God; I say No to attempts to convert Jews to Christianity, since they are already God's covenant people.

3. *God:* I say Yes to the biblical God who shares our plight in suffering love and thereby opens the way for us to love one another; I say No to an all-powerful God

who would thereby be responsible for evil, whether the murder of six million Jews or the unjust death of a single child.

I say Yes to the biblical God as the true God in distinction from false gods; I say No to the false gods, believing that continual No-saying to our most dangerous contemporary false god—uncritical nationalism—is a way of saying Yes to the true God. This means saying No when our government invades other countries, breaks international law, deports political refugees to sure death, supports military dictators, and gives priority to the arms race over the needs of the poor.

I say Yes to the ongoing presence and power of God in the Holy Spirit; I say No to our attempts to limit how the Spirit will act.

4. *Human nature:* I say Yes to the image of God in every person, including migrant workers, women, Sandinistas, and homosexuals; I say No to those who deny that image by rewarding the rich at the expense of the poor, I say No to the church that denies full participation to women by de facto discrimination in jobs, pay, and use of noninclusive language, and I say No to the church that denies ordination to homosexuals, forcing them to lie if they wish to fulfill God's calling to them.

I say Yes to the presence of sin not only in human hearts but in political and economic structures that exalt competition at the price of destroying others; I say No to those who tell us that sin is the monopoly of our enemies.

I say Yes to the transforming power of divine and human forgiveness; I say No to the proposition that we ever move beyond a need for such forgiveness.

I say Yes to God's concern for every human being and the consequent need for society as a whole to provide basic human necessities for all; I say No to those who leave such tasks to the whim of private charities.

5. *The church:* I say Yes to the church that stresses

liberty to the captives; I say No to the church that denies "the cry of the poor" by accepting social structures that violate the poor.

I say Yes to the church that celebrates God's liberating power with bread and wine; I say No to those who do not affirm that accepting food and drink at Christ's Table means ensuring food and drink on all other tables.

I say Yes to the need for the church to take sides; I say No to the church when it claims that political or economic neutrality is possible.

I say Yes to the importance of sharing our faith with others; I say No to sharing built on fear or coercion that promises salvation only to those who verbally acknowledge Jesus as Lord.

6. *Eschatology:* I say Yes to a generous view of the power of God's grace to overcome sin and death; I say No to a belief that reliance on grace can exempt us from the ongoing struggle for justice.

I say Yes to the Kingdom of God as a present possibility in this world; I say No to the Kingdom of God as only a future possibility in another world.

I say Yes to the joy of living in a world where "the mercies of God are fresh every morning"; I say No to any ultimate denial of those mercies.

About the encounter with presbytery: I note only that before my own presentation a former student of mine was unanimously approved, and that I was also approved, but with a smattering of No votes. It made the exercise worthwhile.

I believe we are in the midst of bad times and that they are likely to be worse by the time this volume appears in print. The issue that makes for bad times is the sin most roundly condemned by the Hebrew prophets—the sin of *idolatry*.

Our English word comes from the Greek: *eidōlon* ("idol" or "image") and *latreia* ("service" or "worship");

hence, idolatry is the service or worship of an idol or image. We may understand it to mean *the worship of a false god,* for an idol either takes the place of the god it represents or is a rival for the allegiance we are to reserve for the one true God. None of this is old-fashioned primitive stuff; the New Testament talks particularly about the idolatry of money, the idolatry of the law, and the idolatry of oppressive political power—three "idols" as attractive today as they were in biblical times. As a group of Latin American scholars reminds us, "false gods [or idols] not only exist today but are in good health" (introduction to Pablo Richard et al., *The Idols of Death and the God of Life: A Theology;* Orbis Books, 1983; see also Kosuke Koyama, *Mount Fuji and Mount Sinai: A Critique of Idols;* Orbis Books, 1985, from which some of the above material is drawn). In the pages that follow, the appeal of the idol embodied in the state or nation will be our central concern—an idol for which the biblical term "Caesar" is increasingly appropriate. Our own government appears to me less and less amenable to internal criticism and more and more immune from public accountability—two excellent reasons why it needs challenging in the name of God. Thus the process of saying Yes and saying No is one of sorting out what is really to be rendered to God and what is left for Caesar. And when Caesar begins to act more and more like god (a false god), the need for discrimination between God and Caesar takes a quantum leap.

In the spring of 1985 there was a notable confrontation between the pride of Caesar and the courage of the prophet. The President of the United States decided to honor the war dead in the German cemetery at Bitburg, in itself a compassionate act. But it was shortly discovered that the cemetery contained the remains of forty-nine members of Hitler's SS squad—those who had responsibility for the death camps in which millions of Jews were murdered—and who scarcely deserved honoring.

Rather than acknowledging its mistake, however, the

administration stonewalled and began to justify the visit, even to the point of suggesting that those who ran the camps were as much Hitler's "victims" as those whom they murdered.

At just this time, Elie Wiesel, himself a survivor of the most notorious of the camps, Auschwitz, was scheduled to receive the Congressional Medal of Honor from the President for his literary achievements. In a moment almost unprecedented in American political history, Wiesel, in his acceptance speech before millions of TV viewers, chose to fulfill the ancient prophetic role of "speaking truth to power." In the strongest terms he publicly urged the President to cancel the proposed wreath-laying at Bitburg so that the true victims of Hitler's terror would not be demeaned once again by glorifying their slayers. For Wiesel, to say Yes to truth meant saying No to power.

Power chose not to listen, and the visit was carried out as scheduled. But at the very least the prophetic No was spoken, and millions of viewers gained a new respect for the fact that no Caesar, ancient or modern, is exempt from accountability at the hands of those who claim a higher loyalty.

Christians in Germany in the 1930s faced the necessity of saying Yes to God and No to Hitler, the German Caesar, and their story forms an appropriate launching pad for the present inquiry. To speak of the Germany of Hitler and the America of Reagan within the same volume is not, however, to indulge in comparisons, as though we are now where they were then. That must be clear. But what must be equally clear—and provides the sense of urgency for these pages—is that we are drifting toward a situation when the comparisons would be appropriate.

If I were to lay my greatest fear on the table, it would not be that we are in danger of "sliding down the slippery slope of socialism" (which strikes me as about as low on the list of current American temptations as I can imagine), but that we will slide down another slippery slope toward something that will be less akin to socialism and more akin to "fascism with a friendly face." And since it was the great failure of the German church *to wait too long* before engaging in significant protest, the great challenge to the American church is to avoid that failure and to speak loudly and clearly at the first telltale signs of national idolatry, so that its development can be arrested before it is too late.

It is my conviction that the surest resources for Christians in discovering and combating idolatry are found within the Scriptures, and in an earlier book, *Unexpected News: Reading the Bible with Third World Eyes* (Westminster Press, 1984), I examined biblical passages that in one way or another alert us to its spread. The second chapter here continues this kind of biblical examination, but readers who wish to pursue the biblical resources more fully are referred to *Unexpected News* for the kind of detail that cannot be repeated here.

The remaining chapters contain a sampling, but only a sampling, of issues in which a Yes to the God of the Bible forces us to say a No to false gods of the state who crave our allegiance.

These chapters are not sparing in their criticism of our national life. That is because they spring from a deep faith: a faith first of all in the resources of the biblical heritage to speak to our situation, but a faith also in the resilient power of a democratic society to foster self-criticism that is not disloyal but represents a deep loyalty to all that the nation is meant to be. I ask readers to recall both aspects of that faith if they confront passages that set their teeth on edge.

The No is always for the sake of the Yes.

1

Barmen:
A Test Case in Saying Yes
and Saying No

If May 31, 1934, is not yet a date that elicits instant recognition, it had better begin to do so. And if "Barmen" is not yet a household word, it had better become one. For on May 31, 1934—just over half a century ago—members of the German Confessing Church signed a declaration in the city of Barmen (hence the name Barmen Declaration) that is one of the most important religious documents of our time. It is as relevant now as it was then and it is likely to become more relevant with each passing year. It is a clear example of the practice of saying Yes and saying No.

By May 1934, Hitler was well into the second year of consolidating unlimited power. Faced with his increasing control, most of Germany had capitulated: the business communities, the universities, the cultural groups, and the churches had almost without exception bought into the Nazi vision. Some Christians continued to resist—Franz Jaegerstetter, Martin Niemöller, Dietrich Bonhoeffer, Bishop Lichtenberg, and Fr. Alfred Delp, to name a few—but the church itself was increasingly taken over by the "German Christians," a group that affirmed Hitler as a new Messiah, accepted Nazism's anti-Semitism, and was willing to follow the dictates of the Nazi party. It was largely in reaction to the excesses of the "German Christians" that another group, called the

Confessing Church, was formed, chiefly out of the Lu-
theran and Reformed churches. The Barmen Declaration
was the work of this group, written at its initial synod.
The fine hand of Karl Barth, the Swiss theologian who
was still teaching at Bonn at the time, is evident
throughout, and the document is a good case study of
Barth's contention that theology and politics go hand
in hand.

On first reading, however, the declaration appears
neither political nor dangerous. It seems theological, biblical, ecclesiological, and nonpolitical. Such a reading,
however, is wide of the mark. In the Germany of 1934,
there was no way to make the kind of theological affirmations contained in the document without being extremely
political. We can see this clearly by considering the two
sides of the initial proposition: its affirmation and consequent negation, its Yes and its No. The affirmation
reads:

> Jesus Christ, as he is attested for us in Holy Scripture, is
> the one Word of God which we have to hear and which we
> have to trust and obey in life and in death.

This is good, solid Christian doctrine that most church
people could easily affirm with no expectation that it
would get them into trouble. But we must notice the
strength and cumulative force of the verbs. The affirmation's power is meant to move people *to hear*, but hearing
alone is not enough; it must move them *to trust*, and
trusting is taking what is heard with sufficient serious-
ness to bank one's life on it, to make an act of faith. To
trust means to remain faithful even when the evidence
goes the other way. To trust also includes the need *to
obey*, which involves not only inner commitment but
outer deportment. To obey is to follow through on trust,
being willing to take the consequences. The signers of
the Barmen Declaration knew that the costs might be
high. Realizing that this was not a fair-weather agree-
ment, they acknowledged the need to hear, trust, and

obey "in life and in death." To hear, trust, and obey is to put one's life on the line.

How so? Because to affirm certain things means to deny other things. The declaration's negation, following immediately upon its affirmation, its No in the light of the Yes, makes this clear:

> We reject the false doctrine, as though the Church could and would have to acknowledge as a source of its proclamation, apart from and besides this one Word of God, still other events and powers, figures and truths, as God's revelation.

That still doesn't sound very dangerous. The word "Hitler" occurs nowhere within it, nor in the entire declaration. But no one living in Germany in 1934 could fail to see that the reality of Hitler had called forth the entire document. What Hitler had claimed and gotten from the German people was precisely the acknowledgment that the truth for them *was* found "apart from and besides this one Word of God"—that is, in the Nazi party—and that it *was* in "other events and powers, figures and truths"—that is, the Nazi ideology, its rise to power and its leaders—that Germany's salvation was to be found. "Blood and soil," racial purity, and anti-Semitism were to be accepted as truths. Consequently, to say Yes to Jesus Christ (as the affirmation does) meant to say No to Adolf Hitler and all that he represented (as the negation does).

The same point is succintly made by the title Martin Niemöller gave to a book of sermons published during this period. He called it *Christus ist mein Führer*, Christ is my "Führer," or leader. The use of the word *Führer*, we may be sure, was not inadvert, since everybody in Germany referred to Hitler by that title. To say "Christ is my Führer" was also to say "Hitler is *not* my Führer." And that distinction cost Niemöller seven years in Dachau.

Barmen as a *status confessionis*

Theologians frequently resort to foreign phrases to
make a point (a sin to which I am about to succumb).
They call the kind of times that brought forth Barmen a
status confessionis, meaning "a confessional situation,"
in which the church, in order to be true to itself and its
message, must distinguish *as clearly as possible* between truth and error. There are many times, particularly if public policy is concerned, when Christians may
disagree. American Christians, for example, frequently
disagree about tariff policies or interest rates. But some
issues are so fateful that no disagreement or compromise
is possible. The signatories of the Barmen Declaration
clearly felt they were living in a time when no one and
no church could any longer say, "We affirm both Christ
and Hitler." They had to proclaim, in effect: "The discussion about whether or not we can support Hitler is now
closed. We have rendered our verdict: We cannot. There
is no longer a basis for negotiation." Either/or, not
both/and.

Situations of such clarity are rare and should not be
prematurely or artificially invoked, for they can lead to
terrible acts of spiritual judgment and pride. But there
has been at least one other *status confessionis* in the
church since the time of Hitler. The issue has been apartheid, the forced separation of the races in South Africa.
Until 1982, members of the various Reformed churches
in South Africa had managed to take all sides of the
issue. Some argued that apartheid was consistent with
the Christian gospel, others declared that it was not,
many said that the issue wasn't clear, and the rest said
that the debate was none of the church's business. A
familiar lineup of options. But the injustice and destructiveness of apartheid finally became so obvious that, at
the urging of South African churches that are members
of the World Alliance of Reformed Churches, the latter
body, meeting in Ottawa in August 1982, formally de-

clared apartheid a heresy. As a result, it is no longer possible for members of the World Alliance to affirm the Christian faith and affirm apartheid. The Alliance recognized a *status confessionis*, and a clear either/or was stated: either Christ or apartheid, but not both.

The German situation and our own

As we confront our own nation, we must remember that we live in a religiously pluralistic country, quite different from the Germany of fifty years ago. During the Vietnam years, a number of us gathered to explore the possibility of creating a "Confessing Church" and issuing our own counterpart to the Barmen Declaration, expressing the need to say an unequivocal No to our government's foreign policy because we must say an unequivocal Yes to Jesus Christ. We decided not to do so, largely because we were already working closely with many people in the Jewish community. Rendering our witness in the Christological terms of Barmen would have cut us off from them, and that was a price we were not willing to pay.

Today, as we explore the possibility that we may be approaching a *status confessionis* in which a Yes to Jesus Christ would mean a No to many of our government's policies, we must work in concert with Jews who share our concerns, rather than apart from them. When Christians say that "Jesus Christ is Lord"—meaning that the state and the nation are *not* Lord—we are saying what Jews declare when they give assent to the First Commandment, "You shall have no other gods before me," an assertion we will explore in the next chapter. We must find ways to close ranks with Jews—and indeed with all other persons of goodwill—to speak unitedly about our common concerns. It is one of the shortcomings of the Barmen Declaration that its creators did not see clearly what was happening to Jews in Germany, and thus failed to address the most obscene of all of Hitler's policies.

Do we confront a *status confessionis* in the United States?

Many people would support the notion that in extremely perilous times—the totalitarian world of George Orwell's *1984*, the Germany of the 1930s, and the South Africa of the 1980s—when issues of right and wrong emerge with stunning clarity, there is a place for unequivocal stands. But far fewer would agree that we are close to such times in the United States today.

Because Christians disagree about domestic and foreign policies, the notion that we could take any position along a spectrum of points of view and either baptize or anathematize it, would strike most people as theological imperialism of the worst sort. I might privately believe that my position was the only true Christian one, and I might do all I could to persuade people of its truth, but I would be unjustified in seeking to unchurch or deny the name of Christian to those who disagree with me.

Or is that too benign a scenario? Are we actually facing a *status confessionis*? I believe there are at least two issues forcing us close to the kind of decision demanded of Germans in the 1930s, when saying Yes to God forces us to say No to certain policies and demands of our nation and its leaders.

1. Nuclear weapons? The first of these is the issue of nuclear weapons. I sometimes fear that just as Germans today look back on the early 1930s and say, "How could we have been so blind as not to have seen the peril of Hitler?" so people of a later generation (if, indeed, there is one) will look back on us and say, "How could they have been so blind as not to have seen the peril of nuclear weapons?" The Roman Catholic bishops' recent pastoral letter on nuclear weapons contains an implicit logic that all of us together need to push even farther. The bishops argue that there is no situation in which the *use* of nuclear weapons could be morally permissible. But if to *use* such weapons is wrong, it must also be wrong to *possess* them, since possession tempts powerfully toward use—whether by deliberate decision, technological accident, or human error. And if it is wrong to *use* nuclear weapons and wrong to *possess* them, it must also be wrong to *manufacture* them, since manufacture inevitably means possession, and possession almost inevitably means use.

The bishops' letter does not push that argument to its conclusion, reasoning that, for the moment, possession may be *provisionally* justified if it is used as a basis for sincere negotiations to reduce and finally eliminate all nuclear weapons. If such acts of good faith are not soon forthcoming, however, the bishops might be forced to press the argument all the way, arriving at a *status confessionis* requiring an unequivocal No to nuclear weapons in light of our faith.

The World Council of Churches, at its 1983 Vancouver Assembly, approved a report on "Confronting Threats to Peace and Survival" that seems to push the logic all the way and declare a *status confessionis*. The report is "commended to the churches for study and appropriate action," without in any sense binding them. But the very structure of the section on "nuclear arms, doctrines and disarmament" recapitulates the structure of the Barmen Declaration—first an affirmation of Jesus Christ and then a consequent negation. The first lines of the section follow:

> It would be an intolerably evil contradiction of the Sixth Assembly's theme, "Jesus Christ—the Life of the World," to support the nuclear weapons and doctrines which threaten the survival of the world. . . .
> We believe that the time has come when the churches must unequivocally declare that the production and deployment as well as the use of nuclear weapons are a crime

against humanity and that such activities must be condemned on ethical and theological grounds. . . .

Nuclear deterrence, as the strategic doctrine which has
justified nuclear weapons in the name of security and war
prevention, must now be categorically rejected as contrary
to our faith in Jesus Christ who is our life and peace.
Nuclear deterrence is morally unacceptable because it re-
lies on the credibility of the *intention to use* nuclear
weapons: we believe that any intention to use weapons of
mass destruction is an utterly inhuman violation of the
mind and spirit of Christ which should be in us. (David
Gill, ed., *Gathered for Life*, p. 75; Wm. B. Eerdmans, 1984)

Such an unequivocal stance is risky. But the Confessing Church's 1934 stand was also risky. Risk is part of
the authentic Christian vocabulary and life-style.

2. The national security state? But we have not yet
finished with Barmen's challenge to us. There is another
portent that increasingly demands our No if we are to
continue to say Yes to God. This portent is a reality
increasingly referred to as the national security state.
We will consider it in more detail in chapter 4, but it is
important to raise the issue here, since it lies at the
heart of the concern in every chapter. We can do so by
reference to a description of the national security state,
George Orwell's grisly novel *1984*. The book takes us
into a hideous world of thought control, informers, and
torture. The essential government propaganda indus-
tries, Newspeak and Doublethink, exist to make syntac-
tical and logical sense out of three slogans that dominate
the book and the world it describes: War Is Peace, Freedom Is Slavery, Ignorance Is Strength.

Many people believe that *1984* describes life in the
Soviet Union, and Big Brother certainly bears a re-
semblance to Uncle Joe Stalin. Others see it as a description of the German Third Reich, defeated by the Allied
armies even as the book was germinating in the author's
mind. Still others, myself included, view it as a descrip-

tion of tendencies that are further advanced in our own society than we want to believe.

Juxtaposing Orwell's book and the Barmen Declaration is important, for if we are to stand against evidences of the Orwellian world that are already apparent, important resources for doing so will be found in the themes of Barmen. If we affirm Barmen, we will be forced to challenge almost every aspect of the Orwellian universe.

If we are concerned about drifting into a *1984* world, then Barmen provides a timely warning, for its tragedy was that it came too late. By the time of its creation, Hitler had so consolidated his power that the only witness against him still possible was martyrdom. The telltale signs had not been taken seriously enough soon enough. We are not yet living within the crudely totalitarian and oppressive atmosphere of Orwell's world, but if there are subtle signs that we may be moving in its direction, it is vital to reflect on the meaning of Barmen, in order to speak and act while there is still time.

Let us use the Orwellian slogans just cited to indicate items on the horizon that must be challenged. We will be pursuing them in more detail in subsequent chapters.

Recent events in the United States remind us of *1984*'s slogan, War Is Peace. When the United States engaged in a clear act of war, the military invasion of Grenada, the President repeatedly described it as not an invasion but a "rescue mission." He insisted on this distinction during a news conference, chastising reporters who were so shortsighted and politically biased as to call it an act of war. No, he repeated, it was a rescue of medical students, an act of *peace* (even though, as we discovered when the government-imposed censorship was lifted, the medical students had been in no danger and did not need to be "rescued").

Similarly, it is a consistent part of administration rhetoric that we are *not* engaging in war in Central America, even though we have mined harbors, bombed oil supplies, and provided massive military supplies and tactical help to Honduras, El Salvador, and the Nicaraguan *contras*. The rhetoric in this case is no more convincing than in the earlier dubbing of missiles of first-strike nuclear capability as "Peacekeepers." All this is Orwellian Doublespeak. Our leaders are beginning to tell us that war is peace.

We are also increasingly reminded of the *1984* slogan Freedom Is Slavery. We are told that if we debate too much and question too much, those very expressions of freedom will make us vulnerable to the enemy and lead to our enslavement. Consequently, such freedoms must be held in check. A good example of such logic is a 1983 piece of White House-initiated legislation mandating that all public officials who have had access to classified materials and who want to comment on public affairs, either now or in the future, must obtain governmental clearance for their remarks ahead of time. The provision applies not only while they are in office but *for the rest of their lives*. This provides a powerful weapon to those in public office to forestall knowledgeable criticism by those best informed to provide that service. What could be more threatening to healthy discussion and evaluation in a democracy than such a law? And even though public outcry caused enforcement of the legislation to be put on hold, it was not rescinded, and thousands of public officials have already agreed to abide by it.

The *1984* slogan Ignorance Is Strength also finds echoes in our time. We are told that the government must not let its people know too much or its dominance in the world will be endangered. A recent example of this attitude was the administration's refusal to let the press cover the invasion of Grenada, a decision we will examine more fully in chapter 5. For four days we experienced total news management and governmental censorship. News favorable to the administration's position was shared, news unfavorable was either suppressed or falsely reported. It was impossible for citizens to assess, criticize, or support the administration's actions from an informed standpoint.

Those four days provided a glimpse of the society Orwell envisioned. The lack of public outcry in the face of such manipulation was astonishing.

Paranoia or preview?

As I was drawing the above parallels I stopped to ask myself, Isn't this all rather paranoid? Aren't these parallels overdrawn and even hysterical? But just when I had almost persuaded myself that some blue-penciling was in order, another sequence of events occurred that convinced me that my tone, rather than being more muted, should become more emphatic.

The sequence began with an address by President Reagan at Georgetown University. The President complained that Congress was hampering his attempts to carry out foreign policy, challenging his decisions publicly, and even withholding funds from activities he deemed essential. While he conceded that there should be debate *before* decisions were made, he felt that once the administration had embarked on a policy, everyone should close ranks behind him. No more criticism, in other words. A high-ranking official, Robert McFarlane, then proposed that if members of Congress disagreed with the administration's policy, they could send private letters to the White House or the State Department but should not voice their criticism publicly.

That was bad enough, but there was worse to come. Shortly after this it became public knowledge *(a)* that our government had been illegally mining Nicaraguan harbors, *(b)* that the President had personally endorsed the project, and *(c)* that he had done so without notifying the proper congressional committees, as he is required to do. All this had been happening while Reagan and his spokespersons were *insisting that there should be no*

public disagreement with administration policy once embarked upon. The Congress, and all of us, were being
asked to give approval to illegal actions.

When the facts were known, and Nicaragua had filed
a complaint with the World Court asking for a judicial
hearing and judgment against the United States, the
administration responded that it would no longer recognize the jurisdiction of the World Court, a decision we
will examine in chapter 6.

Such an attitude, if unchecked, grows into a mentality
that says, "We are above the law. We are not accountable to our own government or to the World Court or to
the rules of international law. We will accuse those who
challenge us, even in Congress, of making us weak and
destroying our ability to stand tall. We are entitled to a
blank check signed by the total electorate."

In the face of this, we come back to Barmen's claim
that there is only "one Word of God which we have to
hear and which we have to trust and obey in life and in
death." For Christians, that Word is Jesus Christ. For
Christians and Jews it is the God of Sinai, the God of the
prophets, the God of the Hebrew Scriptures. For neither
Jews nor Christians is the Word we have to "hear . . .
trust and obey" the leadership of a political party or an
administration. And in the name of the God of Barmen
and Sinai we must protest today, as the signers of the
Barmen Declaration did yesterday, when our leaders
begin to say, "Hear, trust, and obey *us*. We'll tell you
what to think. We'll decide what information you should
have. If we withhold information, it is for your own
good. If our public arguments don't make sense, be assured that there are reasons behind them that we can't
really share with you."

When government officials begin to say such things,
that is the time for challenge, because when a government thinks in this way it is beginning to play God. It is
identifying itself with what Barmen calls the "other

events and powers, figures and truths" that are trying to elicit unquestioning and docile loyalty. The taste of such identification is a heady thing.

As that begins to happen in our time, our response, like the Barmen response, must be No, because we have already said Yes to the one Word of God whom we have to hear, trust, and obey, in life and in death.

Items for Reflection

---

1. The chapter suggests that we may be moving toward a *status confessionis* in two areas: nuclear weapons and the national security state. How much are these mutually interdependent? What other areas of our public life may demand an unequivocal Yes or No?

2. Are there counterparts to apartheid in our society? (See further chapter 7.) What are the characteristics of apartheid, elsewhere or in our own society, that demand unequivocal condemnation when other social sins are not similarly condemned?

3. Is it fair to compare portents in our society to realities in Orwell's society? Can we improve our own society if we subject it to such a steady barrage of criticism?

4. How far should we trust our political leaders when they tell us that certain information must be withheld from us? Are they entitled to embark on national policies when only a small number of people have been consulted? Is it right that once a policy has been determined, public criticism should cease?

5. Can we expect those in positions of national leadership to take the opinions of church people into account? How can such dialogue be carried on?

6. Find examples of contemporary idolatry that illustrate the following definition by Paul Tillich: "Idolatry is the elevation of a preliminary concern to ultimacy. Some-

thing essentially conditioned is taken as unconditional, something essentially partial is boosted into universality, and something essentially finite is given infinite significance" (*Systematic Theology*, Vol. 1, p. 16; University of Chicago Press, 1951).

2

On Rendering
to God and Caesar:
A Series of Biblical Excursions

We have established, with some help from the Confessing Church, that our task is to say Yes to the true God and No to the false gods. We still need to establish the nature of that true God, so that it will be the true God to whom we are saying Yes, not some skillfully disguised version of a false god. Four biblical excursions can help us.

God's curriculum vitae (Exodus 20:1-3)

When we apply for a job, our prospective employer almost always wants a curriculum vitae, a document that describes who we are and what we have done so far. "Here are my credentials, here is why you should take me seriously," is what a curriculum vitae proposes to demonstrate.

The history of philosophy is full of attempts to create a curriculum vitae for God and persuade us that the existence of God can be proved or disproved, while the history of theology is full of attempts to describe the true God (whose existence is already assumed) by using such words as omnipotence, omniscience, omnipresence, or love.

These philosophical and theological attempts have not met with notable success. Part of the reason may be that no one can create a curriculum vitae for someone else; it must be done by the one being described. Question: Has God ever provided a divine curriculum vitae, where God said, in effect, "Here are *my* credentials, here is why you should take *me* seriously"? Answer: Yes.

The context of the answer is the following: The Israelites have fled from a tyrant who was playing god over their lives—a kind of Hitler before Hitler—the Pharaoh of Egypt. They are now wandering all over the Sinai peninsula in a state of utter confusion, desperately needing some marching orders. Their leader, Moses, goes up Mt. Sinai and comes back with some very specific instructions—ten of them—complete with a preface. The preface is important. For before getting into the specifics of how the Israelites are to deal with sexual relations and private property, there is a divine curriculum vitae, laying out who God is and why the marching orders must be taken seriously.

The brevity of God's curriculum vitae is like a breath of fresh air to those accustomed to reading piles of vitae with their endless accounts of self-enhancement. It does not begin, "Here are five reasons to prove that I am the creator of the universe, so shape up," or, "I will provide ample evidence in the next few paragraphs that I am the author of beauty, so look around and be amazed," or even, "For all of you philosophy buffs, I am that being than which no greater can be nor be conceived." Instead, it goes, in its entirety, "I am the Lord your God, who brought you out of the land of Egypt, out of the house of bondage" (Ex. 20:2). Period. At the moment when a confused Israel needs overwhelming insight and reassurance, one sentence must suffice. But what a sentence. . . .

If we expand it into a number of sentences, it comes out something like this: "I am the God who is always on the scene, and when injustice is being done, I see to it that the injustice stops and is replaced by justice. Look at your own situation. You were slaves in Egypt, you were in the 'house of bondage,' unable to control your own lives; and instead of asking you to find me in beautiful sunsets or books of philosophy, I worked with you to free you from that bondage. So when you think of justice, or freedom, or liberation, think of me, because I am in the midst of all those things. They are who I really am."

Only after the curriculum vitae do the marching orders come. The first of them is the most important and contains implicitly all that is spelled out explicitly in the remaining nine. It goes, in another example of admirable brevity: "You shall have no other gods before me" (Ex. 20:3).

The big temptation, to the Israelites and to us, is always to have "other gods" at the center of life. In the insecure situation of the Israelites, for example, the big temptation was to make "security" their god, and some of them were already arguing that way. "Better to go back to slavery in Egypt," they were saying, "where at least we got three square meals and a place to sleep, than enjoy the freedom to starve to death in the wilderness. If this is freedom, who needs it?"

But God challenges them to avoid the cop-out of becoming nostalgic about a terrible past. "You shall have no other gods before me" means "You are to say Yes to me and No to the other gods, even if they have names like 'security-in-the-presence-of-tyrants.'" It is the message of Barmen three thousand years ahead of time: Yes to God means No to tyranny. Pharaoh and Hitler are carbon copies of each other. Ditto for Caesar, as we will soon discover.

How are the hearers supposed to respond to such a message? It comes to something like this: God is saying, "Since justice is at the top of my agenda, it had better be at the top of your agenda too. For if you 'have no other gods before me,' if you say Yes to me, that means saying Yes to justice, and *that* means saying No to the false gods of injustice, whether their names are Pharaoh

or Caesar or Hitler or gas chambers or apartheid or
neutron bombs or the national security state."

On rendering to Caesar
(Matthew 22:15–22; Mark 12:13–17; Luke 20:20–26)

The Jews made it out of the desert and into the promised land by following that advice. But they gave enough
attention to the "other gods" so that their history was
checkered with rebuffs as well as successes. At the time
of our second biblical excursion they are once again in
"the house of bondage," although the head of state is no
longer Pharaoh but Caesar. Different name, same problem. In a situation where Caesar is calling the shots, and
God is not about to roll back the waters of any local Red
Seas, how are people to figure out what they owe Caesar
and what they owe God?

There is a fascinating, if tantalizing, biblical episode
that deals with this problem, described in almost identical language in the three Synoptic Gospels. The scene is
Jerusalem during the last hectic week of Jesus' ministry.
The authorities are trying *(a)* to destroy his credibility,
(b) to undermine his base of popular support, and *(c)*, if
those tactics fail, to "neutralize" him, which means (as
we have learned from a recent CIA-sponsored manual
on how to defeat the Nicaraguan leaders) to murder him.

It is still early in the week, and things have not yet
come to a head, so the authorities first try guile against
Jesus. They pretend "to be sincere" (Luke 20:20) in order
to "entangle him in his talk" (Matt. 22:15) or "entrap
him" (Mark 12:13), so that he will speak rashly enough
for them to "deliver him up to the authority and jurisdiction of the governor" (Luke 20:20). The opening move is
clever; they seek to ingratiate themselves by flattery
and catch him off guard—"We know that you are true,
and teach the way of God truthfully" (Matt. 22:16)—before throwing him the conversational ticking bomb, "Is
it lawful to pay taxes to Caesar, or not?" (Matt. 22:17).

This apparently innocent question is not innocent at all, and the interrogators know it. If Jesus says, "Yes, it is lawful to pay taxes to Caesar," they will have him entangled in an intricate web of church-state relationships from which he can hardly hope to escape, and his answer will be co-opted by the Jerusalem chapter of the Moral Majority and all the other flag-wavers, as well as costing him the support of the crowd, who not only dislike taxes in general but Caesar's taxes in particular. But if Jesus says, "No, it is *not* lawful to pay taxes to Caesar," he will be guilty of "aiding, counseling, and abetting" civil disobedience and the breaking of Caesar's law; and Caesar, like the United States Department of Justice, has efficient ways of dealing with such subversion—as Jesus himself discovers approximately forty-eight hours later when they issue him a one-way ticket to Golgotha.

So it is strictly a no-win situation the questioners thrust on Jesus: he will be damned if he does and damned if he doesn't.

They have forgotten one thing, however: Jesus knows how to play dialectical hardball with the best of them. First of all, he has developed enough street smarts to recognize exactly what is going on—a fact all the Gospel accounts recognize: he is "aware of their malice" (Matt. 22:18), he knows "their hypocrisy" (Mark 12:15), he perceives "their craftiness" (Luke 20:23). Consequently, he promptly demonstrates that he can give as good as he gets. After warming up by calling them "hypocrites," a pejorative characterization that means "play actors" (i.e., those who pretend to be other than they truly are), he asks for a coin. The request seems harmless enough, so a coin is forthcoming. And then it's question time again, but this time it's Jesus who is asking the not-so-innocent question. Pointing to the image on the denarius, Jesus asks, "Whose likeness and inscription is this?" The game is still elementary; they know the right answer: "Caesar's." And then comes the punch line: "Render to

Caesar the things that are Caesar's and to God the things that are God's" (Mark 12:17; cf. Matt. 22:21; Luke 20:25).

There is no way the opposition can twist that response so as to get Jesus in trouble. Just when they think they have him in a corner, he not only wriggles out but in three swift conversational gambits he has *them* in a corner, from which they can only escape by sinking through the floor: "When they heard it, they marveled; and they left him and went away" (Matt. 22:22). Luke, not one to pull his reportorial punches, tells us in a moment of admirable candor that they failed because "they were not able in the presence of the people to catch him by what he said" (Luke 20:26). Jesus wins the encounter hands down.

But now we have to ask ourselves: Just *what* did Jesus win? He bought a little time for himself (a few days at most, for they nailed him on a "subversion" charge later in the week); he gave his followers the satisfaction of seeing their leader outmaneuver the brightest and best of the legal crowd; and he enunciated a Splendid Principle, "Render to Caesar the things that are Caesar's, and to God the things that are God's."

But we have to acknowledge that, like most Splendid Principles, this one is a little short on practical help in making day-to-day decisions. Conventional interpreters and TV evangelists, to be sure, routinely offer the episode and the Splendid Principle as a theological defense of the status quo: Pay your taxes, stay out of trouble, give Caesar his due (which is whatever Caesar wants, from more MX missiles to "star wars" technology), and go to church on Sunday, which is how you give God *his* due (conventional interpreters and TV evangelists are routinely at home with sexist language).

But that is too easy—bland at best, reactionary at worst. The verse actually lets loose a torrent of concerns that cascade into our lives and focus a question the verse does not ask but insists that *we* both ask and answer.

Before stating the question, let us note that this is typical of the way Jesus taught. He did not leave us an ethical handbook in which we could "look up the answers" and find the particular one that fits our immediate situation. Instead, he provided materials and resources with which we could make our own decisions, which are the only kind of ethical decisions worthy of the name. So the verse demands that we ask yet another question and answer it ourselves: "Just which things are Caesar's and appropriately to be rendered to Caesar, and which things are God's and appropriately to be rendered to God?"

And while Christians will continue to answer that question in different ways, *it is the debate over that question that is the heart of the matter.* For two things are constantly happening in this struggle between our allegiance to God and to Caesar: first, *our* temptation is frequently to render to Caesar a great many things that should be rendered only to God; and second, *Caesar's* temptation is always to want to be God and thereby claim our total allegiance. And in a world where those two temptations often coincide, saying Yes to God and No to Caesar can become a very lonely business.

For when we begin to respond to the command from Sinai to forsake the "other gods" of security and nationhood for the sake of the God of justice, and when we also take seriously that rendering allegiance to God means disavowing that kind of allegiance to Caesar, we find ourselves in quite a bind. Most of the rest of the world want us to serve those other gods and bow the knee to Caesar. "Don't be different," they warn us; "go along with the crowd. Who do you think *you* are to have some inside track denied to the rest of us?" If we are tenacious enough in trying to be loyal to the God of justice, our friends may shun us, our jobs may be threatened. We may be perceived, in Jürgen Moltmann's phrase, as "traitors to our class" and obviously unpatriotic. "America!" we are told. "Love it or leave it."

It is as though we were no longer at home with a past that had previously given us assurance and a sense of identity. It is as though we were living in a foreign land, surrounded by people speaking a different language (even though we understand the words). How do we handle that?

"Singing the Lord's song in a foreign land" (Psalm 137)

It may be some initial consolation to discover that we are not the only ones who have felt that way. Long ago, when the Jews, exiled from their homeland, were forced to settle in far-off Babylon, they raised the same plaintive cry: "How shall we sing the Lord's song in a foreign land?" (Ps. 137:4). How can we worship the true God in a land where only the worship of idols is approved? The cry became a song that found its way into the Jewish songbook, the Psalter. It is a very human song, one that later generations usually ignore because of the harsh judgments in the last two verses. But it offers a catalog of responses to disaster that provide a checklist as we too grapple with the dilemma of living in a world where we often feel like aliens.

1. Sometimes, in a strange situation, all we seem able to do is *weep* (Ps. 137:1). Our memories of the past are so devastating, and the actualities of the present are so discouraging, that we have no courage to face the future. We feel so cut off, and find our ordinary supports so weak, that we break down in the face of multiple hardships.

2. Weeping is at least an honest accounting of how we feel. It may alternate with *silence* (v. 2), a refusal to face the devastation around us. We "hang up our lyres," unwilling to sing or play, trying to bury the pain and shove it inside.

3. Sometimes others demand that we *pretend* (v. 3) to be on top of things. "Sing!" they say. "Put on a brave

front; it can't be as bad as you think." Or, "Laugh!" they
say. "Don't go sour on us. For our sake at least, put on
a stiff upper lip." But, as we all discover, we can pretend
only so long.

4. When the above approaches only make matters
worse, we are overcome with *devastation* (v. 4). The
initially poignant question, "How shall we sing the
Lord's song in a foreign land?" is reduced to a rhetorical
question whose answer has already been determined; we
can't "sing the Lord's song in a foreign land." Devastation.

5. But devastation is not the last word. Amazingly,
there is a change of mood. The psalmist apparently discovers that from devastation there is no way left but
up. There is a way to cope with the devastation: it is the
way of *memory* (vs. 5–6). In verse 1, "remembering
Zion" led only to desolation and weeping. But now, memory presents a ringing challenge: we are to summon our
memories by writing them down so that they will endure
and others can be empowered by them. Our right (i.e.,
writing) hand deserves only to "wither" if we forget the
greatness of the past, symbolized by Jerusalem (v. 5);
not only that, our voices should be struck mute (v. 6) if
we do not share the heritage now being scorned by those
who hold us in captivity. Message for the 1980s: If we
today are timid, let us remember Barmen, just as those
at Barmen remembered Jesus, who remembered the
prophets, who remembered God.

6. In a rallying mood, the psalmist not only calls upon
people to remember one another but calls upon *God to
remember also* (v. 7), to continue to be the God whose
mighty deeds in the past become the hope and assurance
of mighty deeds in the future. "If God be for us," as Paul
put it many centuries later, "who can be against us?"
(Rom. 8:31, KJV).

7. And then the whole thing comes unraveled. For to
what end are the memories to be enlisted? For *revenge*
(vs. 8–9). "We will, by God, get even," the psalmist
gloats. "We will exact vengeance, we will pay them back

and then some, by bashing out their children's brains at the nearest handy rockpile."

Reprehensible, we quickly conclude. But—let's confess it—there are times when we feel like that too, though we probably don't advertise the fact so publicly, times when we are so outraged at what is going on that we can understand exactly where the psalmist is coming from, and agree in the very marrow of our bones, for a few moments at least, that no retribution, however terrible, would be inappropriate as a way of evening the score.

Once we have acknowledged that feeling, however, and recognized how utterly "human" it is, we must—on the basis of what we know elsewhere in the Bible of God—repudiate those last four vengeful lines (vs. 8–9). This is the eye-for-an-eye morality that the Bible elsewhere repudiates. We cannot by any stretch of the imagination, or any manipulation of the biblical message, transform these final lines into a *divine* command that reads, "God orders you to destroy the children of your enemies."

So we will have to take a final biblical excursion to learn more creative ways of using our memories—memories of the God of justice whom Moses encountered on Mt. Sinai—and discerning the sort of conduct such a God expects of us.

The word for the future is: reversal
(Isaiah 61:1–4)

The setting of Isaiah 61:1–4 is also a time of exile and mourning. Once again the Jews are in captivity. Once again they have to ask how to "sing the Lord's song in a foreign land." They must have gone through all the human emotions Psalm 137 describes, including the temptation to settle for revenge. But the Isaiah passage concludes differently, and there seem to be two reasons for this: (1) The faith of the writer is anchored not in the hatred of enemies but in the greatness of God, the God of justice celebrated in the preface to the Ten Commandments (compare Ex. 20:2 and Isa. 61:8). (2) Since the writer believes that God is just, it is possible to hope for a new situation in which the present injustice is overcome, for injustice does not have the last word; God has the last word. And since we too live in a time of manifest injustice throughout the world, we are called to affirm with the Isaiah writer that since God is just, justice will ultimately prevail in God's universe and the present situation of injustice can be reversed. We are to be enlisted in the struggle to bring that about.

The first two verses of the Isaiah passage are familiar to readers of Luke 4:16–30, for this is the Old Testament passage Jesus reads and comments on in the synagogue in Nazareth. (The episode is discussed at length in *Unexpected News*, ch. 6.) The verses in both versions speak of *reversal*—good tidings to afflicted folk, the binding up and healing of broken hearts, liberty to captives, freedom to prisoners.

But the Isaiah passage, longer than the portion quoted in Luke, extends the good news of reversal even more widely—to "all who mourn" (Isa. 61:2), to all who feel threatened, or down and out, or weak, or sad (v. 3). Things will be turned around—all over the place, wherever we look. There will be "a garland instead of ashes"; there will be "the oil of gladness instead of mourning"; people will be clothed in a "mantle of praise" instead of a "faint spirit" (v. 3). Where they can now see only ruins, they will be empowered to "build up the ancient ruins." Where there were only ruined cities, "they shall repair the ruined cities" (v. 4). They shall also "raise up the former devastations . . . the devastations of many generations" (v. 4). New things will come out of the old, and it is their job, sustained by God, to bring it about. No wonder they will be called "oaks of righteousness" (v. 3).

Here is an almost unparalleled message of hope, inserted in the midst of an almost unparalleled time of hopelessness. The present course of events, they are told, need not go unremittingly toward destruction. *There can be reversals.*

Apparently the people at the time of writing believed that that could happen, that reversals were possible. It takes some doing to replicate their mood today. We have plenty of evidence for a gloomy scenario, and precious little evidence to suggest aligning ourselves with this exultant writer. How could we take that message seriously as a message for us? The passage gives us two clues.

The first clue is *explicit* and is found at the very beginning. Is this passage the shallow optimism of some romantic poet who simply can't face reality? No. The writer says otherwise and makes a bold claim: "The Spirit of the *Lord* is upon me, because *God* has appointed me to preach good tidings to the afflicted" (Isa. 61:1, adapted). The author claims divine authority for the message: these are the things *God will oversee*. It's an all-or-nothing claim, either sober reality or egregious nonsense. We are allowed to take our pick.

The second clue is *implicit* and is found throughout. If this is what God wills, then we are not to sit back and wait for God to bring it all to pass but to align ourselves with those concerns, to make God's concerns our own. To say Yes to God, in the context of this passage, means to say Yes to God's purposes as well, by working for their fulfillment. God wants justice? Then act justly. God wills the building up of ancient ruins? Then break out the block and tackle, the cement mixers, the trowels, and get to work. God wants comfort for those who mourn? Then dispense comfort yourself, share a new vision and a new hope. . . .

Items for Reflection

1. Indicate ways in which the commands "You shall have no other gods before me" and "Render to Caesar the things that are Caesar's, and to God the things that are God's" are variations on a single theme. How else might we state that theme?

2. Is it distorting the evidence to talk about world leaders today in the same breath with Pharaoh, Caesar, or Hitler? What are the commonly shared characteristics of those with great power? What are the differences?

3. How could two writers, both living in exile and among ruined hopes, come to such different conclusions as the writers of Psalm 137 and Isaiah 61?

4. Reflect on the following incident in the light of the conclusion of Psalm 137:

During the war of liberation in Nicaragua, Tomás Borge, the present Minister of the Interior, was captured and severely tortured. After the war, the new government brought captives to trial who had committed war crimes. Borge's torturer was apprehended in this group, and the tribunal gave Borge the privilege of passing sentence on him. In a situation where revenge would have been expected, Borge said to his torturer, "You will have to live with the consequences of what you have done. My 'revenge' on you is to forgive you."

5. Are the hopes expressed in Isaiah 61 realistic? What resources are available to the author (and to us) to guard against premature discouragement? In what ways could the perspective of Isaiah 61 help us to have a clearer understanding of saying Yes and saying No?

3

The "Moral Madness" of the Prophets and the Necessity for Outrage

We have discovered that the Bible has many resources for learning to say Yes and No. Within the Bible there is a further resource to which we must now give attention: the prophetic tradition. When things got tough, and there was need for an unambiguous word from the Lord, God would raise up a prophet to speak that word. Fortunately God continues to do so, and we have been reintroduced in our time to the prophetic tradition by one who exemplified it, Abraham Joshua Heschel, who until his death in 1972 was professor of ethics and mysticism at the Jewish Theological Seminary of America—a title that symbolized a unity at the very core of his being.

Divine pathos

In *The Prophets* (Harper & Row, 1962), Heschel stresses "divine pathos," which he defines as "combining absolute selflessness with supreme concern for the poor and exploited" (p. 271). He claims that this "can hardly be regarded as the attribution [to God] of human characteristics," for there is no human being, not even in the Bible, who could be characterized the way the Bible characterizes God: "merciful, gracious, slow to anger, abundant in love and truth, keeping love to the thousandth generation." Such pathos, then, "is a genuine insight in God's relatedness to man, rather than a projection of human traits on divinity."

To the degree that these are even occasionally characteristics of our human nature, Heschel insists, to just that degree we are endowed with attributes of the divine. His conclusion—characteristically reversing our usual ways of thinking—is that "God's unconditional concern for justice is not an anthropomorphism. Rather man's concern for justice is a theomorphism" (pp. 271–272). In less technical language, concern for justice is not a human trait we project onto God; rather, concern for justice is a divine trait, and to the degree that we embody justice, God takes form within us. Here is a new approach to ethics.

"Radical amazement"

It is from this perspective that Heschel urges us to approach the world in an attitude of "radical amazement." This does not mean turning away from everyday experience (a temptation of certain brands of mysticism), but rather *being open in a new way to every aspect of experience.* There are three ways, he writes, in which we may respond to the world around us: "We may exploit it, we may enjoy it, we may accept it in awe" (Heschel, *God in Search of Man,* p. 34; Farrar, Straus & Giroux, 1955).

Our generation has reached new heights (or depths) in its ability to *exploit* the earth—a fact Heschel noted long before ecological consciousness became fashionable. It is an advance to suggest that we *enjoy* nature rather than exploiting it, since those who enjoy usually take care not to exploit the objects of their enjoyment. But Heschel pushes us farther. Unless we not only enjoy the world but also *accept it with awe,* we will continue to debase both the created order and those who live in it.

> To the prophets wonder is a *form of thinking.* It is not the beginning of knowledge but an act that goes beyond knowl-

edge; it does not come to an end when knowledge is acquired; it is an attitude that never ceases. There is no answer in the world to man's radical amazement. (*The Prophets*, p. 46)

Ideas such as this have consequences. Heschel discovered that the great medieval Jewish thinker Maimonides moved "from scholarship to social action, from metaphysics to ethics, from thoughts to deeds." After a long life as a philosopher, Maimonides became a physician. "Preoccupation with the concrete man and the effort to aid him in his suffering is now the form of religious devotion. . . . Contemplation of God and service to man are combined and become one" (Heschel, *The Insecurity of Freedom*, p. 290; Farrar, Straus & Giroux, 1966). And so Heschel concludes:

> In contrast to [Maimonides'] earlier view that man's ultimate perfection is purely intellectual—it does not include either actions or moral qualities, but only knowledge—he now defines man's ultimate end as *the imitation of God's ways* and actions, namely, kindness, justice, righteousness. (Ibid., p. 291)

That we are called upon to imitate God, that our social ethics do not derive from who we are but from what God asks of us, that the Bible is not our theology but God's anthropology—all these make clear that, for Heschel, not only are we called into a partnership with God, but God needs us.

God needs us

God needs us? Here is a place where traditional Christians need to learn from Heschel. There is a famous equation in William Temple's *Nature, Man and God* that goes: the world − God = 0; God − the world = God. Not so, Heschel insists. God minus the world is a God diminished. *God needs us.* The fulfillment of God's intention for the world cannot be accomplished apart from the work of God's children. God has placed us in the midst of an unfinished creation and given us the task of helping to bring it to fulfillment.

> The universe is done. The greater masterpiece still un-
> done, still in the process of being created, is history. For
> accomplishing His grand design, God needs the help of
> man. Man is and has the instrument of God, which he may
> or may not use in consonance with the grand design. (*The
> Insecurity of Freedom*, p. 97)

Heschel contrasts this view with theologies and philosophies that tell us we can do nothing to change the course of history and must accept whatever providence hands out to us. "It was good that Moses did not study theology under the teachers of that message," he comments wryly; "otherwise, I would still be in Egypt building pyramids" (ibid., p. 98).

Bible and race: a case study

In contrast to such fatalistic views is the ongoing biblical story of the struggle to overcome oppression—a story that will continue to be written as long as there is oppression to overcome. Heschel laid it out without equivocation in a talk at the National Conference on Religion and Race in 1963:

> At the first conference on religion and race, the main
> participants were Pharaoh and Moses. Moses' words were:
> "Thus says the Lord, the God of Israel, let My people go
> that they may celebrate a feast to Me." While Pharaoh
> retorted: "Who is the Lord, that I should heed this voice
> and let Israel go? I do not know the Lord, and moreover
> I will not let Israel go."
> The outcome of that summit meeting has not come to an
> end. Pharaoh is not ready to capitulate. The exodus began,
> but is far from having been completed. (Ibid., p. 85)

And then—this is 1963—Heschel comments, "In fact, it was easier for the children of Israel to cross the Red Sea than for a Negro to cross certain university campuses."

The connection between then and now is immediate and relentless. We are not allowed to dwell in the past, contemplating the racial injustice of another era. A look at the Bible plunges us into the present, contemplating racial injustice today.

The same dynamic is at work a year later when Heschel addressed another Conference on Religion and Race. With him, we accompany the Children of Israel as they cross the Red Sea, and we share the sublime joy, the spiritual exaltation, of that event. Not even Ezekiel, Heschel informs us, experienced such a sense of divine glory. Three days later, they find no water. So they murmur against Moses, "What shall we drink?" Heschel reflects:

> The episode seems shocking. What a comedown! Only three days earlier they had reached the highest peak of prophetic and spiritual exaltation, and now they complain about such a prosaic and unspiritual item as water. (Ibid., p. 101)

And then, once again, without a pause, comes the transition from the distant past to the immediate present:

> The Negroes of America behave just like the children of Israel. Only in 1963 [i.e., a year ago] they experienced the miracle of having turned the tide of history, the joy of finding millions of Americans involved in the struggle for civil rights, the exaltation of fellowship, the March to Washington. Now only a few months later they have the audacity to murmur: "What shall we drink? We want adequate education, decent housing, proper employment." How ordinary, how unpoetic, how annoying! (Ibid., p. 101)

Heschel describes the pleasant mood of the time, in which all is going well: The Beatles have been in town, AT&T is about to split its stock, Castro is not causing trouble, and Russia is buying U.S. grain. "Only the Negroes continue to disturb us," he laments ironically, with their cry, "What shall we drink?" (ibid., p. 102).

His contrast between occasional acts of "liberal" identification and the demands of the long haul is severe:

> We are ready to applaud dramatic struggles once a year
> in Washington. For the sake of lofty principles we will
> spend a day or two in jail somewhere in Alabama.
>
> But that prosaic demand for housing without vermin,
> for adequate schools, for adequate employment—right
> here in the vicinity of Park Avenue in New York City—
> sounds so trite, so drab, so banal, so devoid of magnifi-
> cence. (Ibid., p. 102)

But it is just this concern for the trite, the drab, the
banal, the unmagnificent that characterizes Scripture
and the God of Scripture. Heschel has no use for Greek
gods contemplating eternal perfection in another realm;
he offers the prophetic view as an alternative:

> The prophet's field of concern is not the mysteries of
> heaven, the glories of eternity, but the blights of society,
> the affairs of the market place. . . . The predominant
> feature of the biblical pattern of life is unassuming, un-
> heroic, inconspicuous piety, the sanctification of trifles,
> attentiveness to details. (Ibid., pp. 102–103)

Why all this emphasis on the ordinary, the trivial, the
unassuming? Because this is the emphasis of the Bible
and the prophets. "The Hebrew Bible," Heschel reminds
us, "is not a book about heaven—it is a book about the
earth. The Hebrew word *erets*, meaning earth, land,
occurs at least five times as often in the Bible as the
word *shamayim*, meaning heaven" (Heschel, *Israel: An
Echo of Eternity*, p. 146; Farrar, Straus & Giroux, 1969).

In the next chapter we will explore the decision by
Latin American Catholics to make "a preferential option
for the poor," based on God's partiality for the oppressed
which God's children must emulate. Heschel was aware
of all that, years before "liberation theology" appeared
on the scene. "The Bible," he points out, "insists that the
interests of the poor have precedence over the interests

of the rich. The prophets have a bias in favor of the poor"
(*The Insecurity of Freedom*, p. 95).

The prophetic stance: "moral madness"

That prophetic bias is a perspective from which to
learn what is involved in saying Yes and saying No.
Heschel decribes it as "moral madness." In the eyes of
their contemporaries, the prophets were mad. Hosea,
Elisha, and Jeremiah were all considered demented, in-
dividuals who (as is specifically suggested in the case of
Jeremiah) should be put "in the stocks and collars" (*The
Prophets*, esp. pp. 402–403).

We call people "mad" when they see things from a
perspective different from our own. We have a vested
interest in doing so, for if they are right, we are wrong.
Since we do not gladly entertain the notion that we are
wrong, we are more than ready to denounce such people
as crazy, mad fools. To be sure, the prophets *do* engage
in some very strange activities: they call kings to account
for injustice, which is a very unhealthy thing to do in a
royal society; they excoriate religious leaders for being
co-opted, which is equally unhealthy in a society that
allows religious leaders to deal with their own deviants;
they announce the fulfillment of God's will through pagan
leaders, which is considered unpatriotic by leaders of
both church and state; and they even rail against the
God in whose name they speak, a matter that God appears to accept with more forbearance than God's emissaries usually do.

Where the shoe pinches for us—who enjoy the support
of the status quo and thrust aside these rude and uninvit-
ing fellows, insisting that "madness" and "sanity" are
determined by majority consensus—is that we can never
quite get rid of the nagging question: *What if we have it
all backward?* What if the minority viewpoint is the true
one? What if the ones we call "mad" are really sane?
What if their saying Yes to God means saying No to all

those things to which we say Yes? What if *we* are the ones who see the world falsely? Those are not the kinds of questions we like to ponder before going to sleep at night, for they are nightmare producing.

Nonconformity is the only posture to which the prophet can conform. In this, Abraham Heschel resembles his biblical namesake, for it was likewise the task of the earlier Abraham not to conform, not to stay in the land where he "had it made," but, in response to a divine mandate, to depart in ways that made his contemporaries think him a fool. The biblical Abraham destroyed the idols of his father. And that has always been a prophetic task—the destruction of idols, whether nation, race, state, status, even religion. Citing the experience of that earlier Abraham, the present-day Abraham, speaking on "Idols in the Temples," said, "Religion begins as a breaking off, as a going away. It continues in acts of nonconformity to idolatry" (*The Insecurity of Freedom*, p. 67).

A human consequence: moral outrage

If "moral madness" is a way of saying Yes to God, moral outrage is a way of saying No to injustice and indifference. Heschel's writings and speeches explode with the indignation so characteristic of his prophetic forebears. Here he is in the midst of the 1972 presidential campaign, when human priorities were all askew:

> If the prophets Isaiah and Amos were to appear in our midst, would they accept the corruption in high places, the indifferent way in which the sick, the poor, and the old are treated? Would they condone the indifference to gun control legislation that has allowed some of the finest of our national leaders to be shot dead? Would not our prophets be standing with those who protest against the war in Vietnam, the decay of our cities, the hypocrisy and falsehood that surrounds our present administration, even at the highest levels? (Byron Sherwin, *Abraham Joshua Heschel*, p. 7; John Knox Press, 1979)

From the prophetic Yes, Heschel could move powerfully
to the prophetic No:

> Must napalm stand in the way of our power to aid and
> inspire the world?
>
> Our government seems to recognize the tragic error and
> futility of the escalation of our involvement but feels that
> we cannot extricate ourselves without public embarrass-
> ment of such a dimension as to cause damage to America's
> prestige.
>
> But the mire in which we flounder threatens us with an
> even greater danger. It is *the dilemma of either losing
> face or losing our soul.* (Robert McAfee Brown, Abraham
> J. Heschel, and Michael Novak, *Vietnam: Crisis of Con-
> science*, p. 49, italics added; Association Press, 1967)

"To speak about God and remain silent on Vietnam is
blasphemous." At a later point he thunders:

> Has our conscience become a fossil? Is all mercy gone? If
> mercy, the mother of humanity, is still alive as a demand,
> how can we say Yes to our bringing agony to the tor-
> mented nation of Vietnam? (Ibid., p. 56)

The posture even invades his prayers:

> O Lord, we confess our sins, we are ashamed of the in-
> adequacy of our anguish, of how faint and slight is our
> mercy. We are a generation that has lost the capacity for
> outrage. (Ibid., p. 50)

Heschel never "lost the capacity for outrage." During
the war years he spoke to a Stanford University ethics
class. It turned out that a friend of one of the students,
both of whom were Jewish, was producing napalm. The
student asked Heschel what she should say to him. "Go
to him," Heschel replied, with barely concealed trem-
bling of limb, "and tell him that if he continues making
napalm he forfeits the name of Jew. Go to him and tell
him that if he continues to create such things he forfeits
the name of human being. Go to him and tell him that if
he continues to be part of such inhuman destructiveness

he sins against creation and the Creator. Go to him and plead with him to repent and ask for mercy while there is still time to do so."

"Some are guilty, all are responsible"

Probably no phrase occurs more frequently in Heschel's writings than the phrase, "Some are guilty, all are responsible." Heschel is reminding us that while there may be differing degrees of direct involvement in evil, rendering some more guilty than others, there is no point at which any of us may claim total exemption. Some are directly guilty, for example, of the ongoing humiliation of people of color—they pass antiracial laws, or they refuse to enforce existing nondiscriminatory laws, or they openly defy existing laws, or they whip up racial antagonism, or they speak and write gainst minority groups. While *some* are directly guilty of such things, *all* are responsible for their continuing. *Those who acquiesce in the evil done by others bear responsibility for that evil.* Those who remain quiet when the demagogue speaks give their support to the demagogue. Those who remain indifferent to the quiet voices of hatred encourage such voices to speak more loudly. Those who privately deplored the war in Vietnam but did nothing about it were targets for his outrage. Those who were not guilty of dropping antipersonnel weapons on defenseless children but were paying taxes or buying Honeywell stock or refusing to protest such inhumane actions were responsible for the actions done by others.

It is not only true that if we say Yes to God, we must say No to evil. It is also true that if we refuse to say No to evil, we cannot say Yes to God.

The importance of not coming too late

When saying Yes to God means saying No to some part of our society, we have elaborate mechanisms for fudging, such as claiming *(a)* that we do not yet know enough to make an intelligent decision, *(b)* that we *do* know enough to know that the issues are too complicated to make an intelligent decision, or *(c)* that the right time to speak and act has not yet come.

Heschel saw the danger inherent in such excuses. By January 1967, at a meeting in Washington to protest the Vietnam War, he already feared that people of conscience would not speak or act until it was too late. He indicated how this fear replicated his own boyhood fears when he was studying Torah at age seven with a rabbi in Poland. Together they read the Akeda, the story of the sacrifice of Isaac. Heschel reconstructed the scene:

> Isaac was on the way to Mount Moriah with his father; then he lay on the altar, bound, waiting to be sacrificed. My heart began to beat even faster; it actually sobbed with pity for Isaac. Behold, Abraham now lifted the knife. And now my heart froze within me with fright. Suddenly the voice of the angel was heard: "Abraham, lay not thine hand upon the lad, for now I know that thou fearest God." And here I broke into tears and wept aloud. "Why are you crying?" asked the Rabbi. "You know Isaac was not killed."
>
> And I said to him, still weeping, "But Rabbi, supposing the angel had come a second too late?"
>
> The Rabbi comforted me, and calmed me by telling me that an angel cannot come too late.

And then, lifting his eyes from his manuscript and looking directly into our eyes, Heschel concluded:

> An angel cannot come too late, my friends, but we, made of flesh and blood, we may come too late. (*Vietnam: Crisis of Conscience*, pp. 51–52, slightly altered)

I was the next speaker on the program. I have forgotten everything I said. But I have never forgotten that it is possible to come too late.

Items for Reflection

1. Is it excessive to say that "God needs us"? Does this put limitations on what God can do? If the prophets are right that God is the God of justice, what kinds of deeds are we to do in "imitating God"?

2. To what degree are the "moral madness" of the prophets and the necessity for "moral outrage" on our part two ways of talking about the same thing?

3. Heschel challenged the great social sins of his time, racism and Vietnam. Racism is still with us. And while the war in Vietnam is over, we hear much talk today of "other Vietnams." Where are the places today toward which our moral outrage must be directed? (See chapters 6 and 10, if nothing comes to mind.)

4. What are the implications for saying Yes and saying No of acknowledging that the Bible "is not a book about heaven—it is a book about the earth"?

5. What are the social ills today in response to which it can be said that "some are guilty, all are responsible"?

6. Psalm 4:4 counsels us to "be angry, but sin not." How can anger ("moral outrage") be a source of empowerment for social change? Can we distinguish between anger and hatred? Should we not be angered if we see an adult beating a child, or are reminded of the reality of the gas chambers of Auschwitz? Can we give vent to anger in ways that do not simply replicate the evil (beating the beater of the child, or consigning to gas chambers those who consigned the Jews to gas chambers)? Does lack of anger in such situations indicate lack of feeling for the victims?

7. Concerning what issues today are we most likely to postpone taking sides on grounds of presumed ignorance or the need to wait for a better time to act? Is it true that "not to decide is to decide"?

4

Combating the National Security State: "The Preferential Option for the Poor"

The terms "Pharaoh," "Caesar," and "Hitler" have been used so far to identify forces to which we must say No, and we have discovered that the reason for this is that Pharaoh and Caesar and Hitler share a common ambition—they all want to be God; that is to say, they all demand the unyielding loyalty that belongs to God alone. "Give us a blank check," they insist. "Don't hold us accountable to anything or anyone beyond ourselves. And if you try to do so, or threaten us in any way, we will dispose of you."

It might seem, however, as though the concern were now dated, for the Pharaohs and the Caesars lived in long-ago Bible times, and Hitler has been safely dead for forty years.

But false gods do not oblige us by remaining safely dead; they share a unique ability to rise from the dead in new forms. It is to the credit of the Roman Catholic bishops in Latin America, from whom we seek to learn in this chapter, that they have identified contemporary reincarnations of the Pharaoh-Caesar-Hitler syndrome in the form of "the national security state" and have realized that it represents a similar false god to which we must say No.

The doctrine of "national security"

The doctrine of "national security" has some clearly identifiable characteristics, most of which are incarnated in Latin American dictatorships of the right against which Christians have set themselves at great personal peril. (For details, see José Comblin, *The Church and the National Security State*, esp. chs. 4–6; Orbis Books, 1979.) Dictatorships of the left likewise have versions of national security doctrine that are almost identical, save that the "enemy" (see point 5 below) is usually capitalism rather than communism. For the moment we will follow the Latin American formulations of the doctrine. They go something like this:

1. The state is *an end in itself*, and its triumph over other states—all of which potentially threaten it—is the reason for its existence. Other states must be forced to submit to the will of *our* state. The state does not exist for the welfare of people; people exist for the welfare of the state.

2. The human condition is one of *perpetual warfare.* What the naïve call "peace" is only an interlude to regroup for overt conflict, a temporary waging of war by other means. The vigilance of the state against inner challenge or criticism must be especially strong in times of "peace."

3. Since the survival of the state is the absolute goal, *any means* can be employed to ensure that survival. Citizens are expected to inform on neighbors whose motives or actions they suspect of being disloyal; the "secret police" keep a file on all such persons; those who think or act in suspicious or "strange" ways can be tortured to extract information from them.

4. Enforcement of the laws of the national security state is entrusted to *the military*. The army will either be overtly in charge or covertly lurking behind civilian politicians whose tenure in office will be directly proportionate to their subservience to the military's wishes.

5. The universal enemy is *communism*, which can be identified with any group or power that does not agree with the national security state, and can be described as any idea or movement that threatens the power of the state. Thus any challenge, internal or external, can be identified as "communist." An opponent of the state is automatically a communist.

6. Since *the church* has a direct stake in the survival of the national security state as a condition of its own survival, the church is expected to be uncritically pro-state and anticommunist.

The message to the ordinary citizen is clear: Don't rock the boat; don't speak (and especially don't act) in ways that challenge the national security state; don't disagree with the authorities; and, if you are a Christian, bring all the resources of your faith to bear on preserving the national security state against its enemies. Loyal citizens can simultaneously say Yes to God and Yes to the national security state. No problem.

The response of the church

But to an increasing number of Latin American Christians there *is* a problem, and it is forcing them in the name of saying Yes to the God of justice to say No to the national security state. The Roman Catholic bishops, meeting in Puebla, Mexico, in 1979, joined the issue.

They gave much attention to the way in which the rights of the individual are destroyed, noting that "in many instances the ideologies of National Security have helped to intensify the totalitarian or authoritarian character of government based on the use of force, and that this has led to frightful abuses of human rights" (report of Commission I). Commission IV elaborated the abuses against individuals, indicating that when the state "enrolls the individual in unlimited service," this means that "individual freedoms are restructured as they are in any emergency situation." In the national security state, the "normal" situation, as we have seen, is one of "emergency," in which the appropriate doctrine is: Anything goes. In one of the most important insights from Puebla, the bishops noted that when the state "presents itself as an Absolute holding sway over persons, in its name *the insecurity of the individual becomes institutionalized*" (italics added).

But it is in the report of Commission VIII that the most basic critique emerged. For there the bishops noted that the doctrine is really an ideology—that is, a total worldview—which demands uncritical acceptance and the delegation of power to a minority that "suppresses the broad-based participation of the people in political decisions." So the bishops repudiated the national security state as something that "would not be compatible with the Christian vision," for "it puts the people under the tutelage of military and political elites . . . and it leads to increased inequality." (For the full report, see John Eagleson and Philip J. Scharper, eds., *Puebla and Beyond;* Orbis Books, 1979.)

From south to north: applications

Once we have thanked the bishops for their willingness to say No to the doctrine of the national security state in such forthright manner, we next need to ask ourselves what the discussion means for those of us in North America who are likely to view the national security state as something both geographically and ideologically remote from our own experience. Two matters are of critical importance.

First, to a degree that we are reluctant to admit, it is our military, economic, and political power that enables national security states to survive and flourish elsewhere. One of the most consistent examples of a national security state, Somoza's Nicaragua, lasted forty-two years solely because of United States backing. The brutal Pinochet regime in Chile, in power for over a decade, was aided in launching its military coup by the United States and has been assisted by the United States ever since, despite massive violations of human rights. In the case of these and other national security states, their own police have been trained in sophisticated methods of torture at United States police academies in Panama and Washington. So it is not sufficient, in looking at national security states in the world today, to point only to Russia or its satellites for examples. We too bear the moral burden of enabling them to thrive.

Second, we also need to take seriously the emergence of characteristics of the national security state in our own society. While we do not have to cope with military coups or forthrightly fascist administrations, we need to be aware of how vital freedoms can quietly and cumulatively be threatened.

Compared to national security states, for example, there is little torture in our society (though members of minority groups in prisons can document contrary claims), but the fact that our officials teach others how to torture indicates an acceptance, on some official level, of the moral acceptability of such a practice, which, in a time of "emergency," could be used against our own citizens.

The use of governmentally paid spies and informers is not a normal practice at home, but it has recently been employed against church members, ministers, priests, and Roman Catholic sisters to secure evidence to convict them in court of helping political refugees from Central America (see chapter 10 for details).

To take another example, making "communism" everybody's favorite whipping boy is virtually routine procedure for people in American public life, who accuse those who differ with them of being communist-inspired, or at least communist "dupes." This serves to discredit any critique they might offer of governmental policies, without having to confront the substance of the charges.

Even the President employed this device in 1983 to discredit those who supported the moderate notion of a nuclear freeze.

Those are only three characteristics of the national security state that we find in preliminary form in our own society. The appropriate response is not to declare that we have become carbon copies of what we profess to abhor, but to take public note of such straws in the wind, so that they can be ferreted out of our national life before becoming deeply lodged. To say Yes to the God of justice is to say No to all such tendencies, and to work for their removal.

"A preferential option for the poor"

How should the church as a whole react to the dangers of the national security state? The Latin American bishops realize that the time is long past when they can expect to "humanize [the national security state] from within"; to attempt to do so would be to take sides with oppressors who are so entrenched in power that every recruit to their ranks makes their dislodging more difficult.

Where, then, must the church be found? The bishops have a clear answer: standing with the victims, siding with the oppressed. And since in Latin America the victims are especially the poor, the church is called upon (in one of the most memorable phrases and important ideas of Puebla) to make "a preferential option for the poor." The phrase, precisely because it is memorable and important, has been both praised and maligned, and we must be clear about its actual meaning.

To speak of "a preferential option for the poor" is not to speak of an "exclusive" option for the poor, as though God loved only the poor and did not love anybody else, especially the rich. What the bishops are asserting is that in responding to the concern that God has for *all* people, we start toward the fulfillment of that long-range concern by an immediate and initial concern for the poor, working with them and for them. To the degree that the cries of the poor are given priority over the complaints of the rich, the bishops argue, there can be movement toward a society that is more, rather than less, just.

This claim seems unexceptionable in terms of any Christian theology derived from the Hebrew prophets and the teaching of Jesus. It is irrefutable that the Bible expresses a special concern for the poor and downtrodden. (Ample documentation of this claim can be found in such books as Gustavo Gutiérrez, *The Power of the Poor in History* [1983]; J. Severino Croatto, *Exodus: A Hermeneutics of Freedom* [1981]; José Porfirio Miranda, *Marx and the Bible* [1974]; and Pablo Richard et al., *The Idols of Death and the God of Life: A Theology* [1983]— all published by Orbis Books.) Biblical concern seems to operate from the grassroots outward and upward. It is as the poor are empowered, and can articulate their own concerns, needs, and demands, that the struggle for justice for *all* is advanced.

It has escaped much notice that the Puebla documents not only speak of "a preferential option for the poor" but link it to "a preferential option for young people." The two are closely interrelated. In situations of extreme poverty, the greatest losers are the young, who experience hunger, malnutrition, and sometimes outright starvation, living in situations so desperate that they are often caught in the midst of violent upheavals that first terrorize and then destroy them. Once again, to affirm "a preferential option for young people" does not mean that God does not love the elderly or that the church has decided to abdicate concern for them. Rather, it reflects a belief that if the needs of both the poor and the young are given priority, actions that work to their advantage will ultimately redound to the benefit of all.

Whether or not the bishops meant it to be that way, one can hardly imagine a more dramatic challenge to the architects of the national security state than to express "a preferential option for the poor," for the poor are the expendables in the national security state, the unimportant, the marginal, those whose "usefulness" is limited to the degree to which they can be exploited to make things more comfortable for the affluent elite. And as, with the help of the church, the poor begin to gain a voice, they will have to be taken more seriously by those in power. The resulting conflicts, though painful, will begin to challenge the injustices of the national security state.

From south to north: further applications

This may still seem a long way from our own situation, until we realize that the North American Catholic bishops, like their southern counterparts, have indicated that North American Christians must make "a preferential option for the poor" as well. The phrase is used in the first draft of their pastoral letter on the state of the economy, and whether or not the precise wording survives in subsequent revisions—the idea makes conservative Roman Catholics very nervous—the viewpoint it represents is reflective of the document as a whole. At the beginning of their examination of the American economy, and a consideration of changes that might be needed, the bishops state:

> *Our fundamental norm is this: will the decision or policy help the poor and deprived members of the human community and enable them to become more active participants in economic life?* (Para. 21, italics in original)

Two emphases in this declaration are crucial. The *first* is an acknowledgment that the criterion must be what happens to "the poor and deprived members of the human community"—a criterion that flies in the face of the conventional American goal of handsomely benefiting those who rise to the top, without too much concern for the less fortunate. The *second* emphasis is that the criterion is not the need to help or benefit "the poor and

deprived" through acts of charity in which the rich give
handouts to the poor but to "enable them to become
more *active participants* in economic life." This means
seeing to it that society is so organized that "the poor
and deprived" participate themselves in the process of
deciding what goods are needed and how to get them, as
well as participating in their consumption. The point is
of incalculable importance; it safeguards against a paternalistic scheme, in which a few rich decide what is to be
given to the many poor, by insisting that the many poor
play a central role in the decision-making that affects
their own destiny. Only in this way can they cease to be
poor. Human dignity, the bishops recognize, is possible
only for those who play a part in creating their own
futures; if others do it for them, the poor remain pawns
in the power game, judged as unable to contribute to the
meaning of their own lives.

The idea is not new. It goes back at least to a document
of the Second Vatican Council:

> The demands of justice should first be satisfied, lest the
> giving of what is due in justice be represented as the
> offering of a charitable gift. Not only the effects but also
> the causes of various ills must be removed. Help should be
> given in such a way that the recipients may gradually be
> freed from dependence on others and become self-critical.
> (Vatican Council, AA:8)

Each sentence implies a radical approach to the economy, "radical" in the sense of getting at the *radix*
("root") of things, and refusing to let us escape from
concern for the poor by cosmetic changes that do not
really change anything. Whoever wants an agenda for
economic revolution need look no further.

What, in turn, does *this* mean for North Americans?
It probably means more than we are ready to take on.
The Latin American church, after all, is *already* "the
church of the poor," in the sense that it does not have to
go out from its walls and find poor people; they are

already *in* the church. Most North American churches, on the other hand, are not visibly the churches of the poor but the churches of the middle and upper classes. It is chiefly the Pentecostals, black churches, and small sect groups who minister to the poor and have already made "a preferential option" on their behalf.

Despite those sociological realities, the Bible's "preferential option for the poor" is a reality our mainline churches cannot ignore, and the North American bishops' pastoral letter makes it impossible to do so. We must confront our privileged status as those who, whether consciously or not, have made a preferential option for the middle class or for the rich. But if God has a special love for the poor, and *sees the poor as those through whom the good news of the gospel can finally be heard by the rich as well*, then some new priorities are mandatory for the rest of us.

We will need, among other things, to get a clearer understanding of just who constitute "the poor." In the Latin American situation, the most visible poor are the economically poor—those without enough income, food, clothing, housing, and education to live lives of minimal dignity. But when we recognize that "the poor" are *all* the disadvantaged in society, those who for any reason do not have an opportunity for any kind of dignity, we find the net widening. It is just beginning to be perceived by Latin Americans, for example, that women are "doubly oppressed." Not only are they among the most economically deprived, they are grossly exploited in other ways as well—those whose working hours never cease; those who are treated as objects for sexual gratification in a macho culture; those who are denied leadership in church and society solely because of their sex; and so on. And then, just as we begin to discover that this is true of women in our own culture, we make the further discovery that it is not only women but members of all minority groups in our society who likewise suffer the "poverty" of less than fully human lives—Native Americans, Hispanics, gays and lesbians, blacks, and many others. Economic poverty is usually central to the burden of such people, but for even the few who escape it, other crushing burdens remain.

The assertion that it is with such persons that our churches are meant to rally and struggle will necessitate a difficult adjustment for Christians who conceive of their churches as places where people "of their own sort" gather. Similarly difficult will be the realization that more is involved than sharing a bit of their superabundance; what needs to be shared is *power*, and that means moving over and making a genuine place for those earlier excluded. It used to be ecumenically fashionable to say that the task of the church was to be "the voice of the voiceless," and both the World Council of Churches and Pope John Paul II championed the theme. We are now beginning to see that the notion is paternalistic and condescending. If the image is salvageable, it must be reconceived to indicate that the task of the church is to provide a place where the previously voiceless can now speak in their own names.

Politics and economics go together

It may seem as though we have been mixing apples and oranges—politics and economics—and that when we throw in religion we confuse things even more.

But there is no way we can separate them. Pharaoh and Caesar want to control both our political and our economic lives, and they want to do so with the connivance of religion. If the national security state victimizes people through fear and punishment, we have no choice, in faithfulness to the gospel, but to stand with the victims—which is what it means to make "a preferential option for the poor." That does not mean that we have access to specific political programs or economic policies, but it does mean that we have access to the perspective from which political programs and economic policies must be developed. And that is where politics and economics come together from a Christian perspective; both of them are meant to create social relationships that enhance human life and dignity, and both must be challenged when they betray those ends. If one is politically free to speak but is starving to death, that is less than full freedom; while if one has sufficient economic goods but cannot speak critically of the society that provides them, that freedom too leaves much to be desired.

Apples and oranges go together.

Items for Reflection

---

1. Six characteristics of the national security state are described early in the chapter. Which ones are not descriptive of our own society? How seriously should we take the claim that some of them are present?

2. What are the points of greatest contrast between Christian faith and the national security state? For each point in the ideology of the national security state, offer a contrasting Christian affirmation—for example, the Christian view of the state, warfare, ends and means, military power, communism, and the role of the church.

3. Does United States support of national security states make us complicit in their violations of human rights? Is it unpatriotic to accuse our nation of sins we usually lay at Russia's door?

4. How can we affirm simultaneously that God loves *all* people and yet claim that God expresses "a preferential option for the poor"? Can churches do this without becoming divided? How can those who are not poor feel welcome in such a situation?

5. Do bishops, or any church leaders, have the competence to make pronouncements about the economy? Even if they have the competence, do they have the right? Is that the task of laypeople?

6. Is it realistic to suggest that church leaders voluntarily surrender power to those who so far have been voiceless and powerless in voice and the church? What would need to happen in church structures for this to take place?

5

Grenada, Preview of the Future: When Caesar Acts Like God

Grenada. . . . The name has already slipped into the backs of our minds. Whatever it was—a rescue of students? a military invasion? a decisive blow to communism? a moment of national pride? a moment of national shame?—it seems too vague and long ago to be worth recalling. Life moves on. Better to let it rest back there.

But precisely because life moves on, it is *not* better to let it rest back there. It must be re-summoned lest it be ignored. For if there is any bit of our recent history of which it can be said, in the words of George Santayana, that "those who ignore history are doomed to repeat it," it is the military invasion—it *was* an invasion—of Grenada by the United States of America in October 1983.

The original title for this chapter ended with a question mark: "Grenada, Preview of the Future?" But the more the material developed, the clearer it became that a question mark made the title too hopeful. Grenada *is* a preview of the future, and only to the extent that we remember this will we be sufficiently energized to prevent its recurrence.

The invasion of Grenada is a highly visible instance of what increasingly characterizes U.S. foreign policy:

- The use of force instead of law or negotiation

- The use of unilateral decision-making instead of international consultation

- The use of news management and censorship instead of truth

- The use of fear of "communism" instead of national accountability

- The use of ideology and self-interest instead of a policy based on concern for all

What this means theologically (as we shall see later) is that the U.S. invasion of Grenada is an example of Caesar trying to act like God and thereby becoming a false god—a god who claims an unchallengeable right to do whatever it pleases and demands unquestioned support for whatever it does. It is the beginning of a North American version of the national security state.

Our government acted in at least four ways during the Grenada invasion that demand a No on our part, if we are to continue to say Yes to the God of justice.

1. *The invasion was both a unilateral and an illegal action,* showing lack of regard both for the concerns of other nations and for the laws and treaties that govern our dealings with those nations. Mr. Reagan did not even consult the Prime Minister of Great Britain, whose territory (as part of the British Commonwealth) we invaded, let alone other world powers, before giving the order to invade. Domestically, not even the United States Congress was consulted, nor were leading members of Mr. Reagan's own party. The decision was made unilaterally by a tiny handful.

As for illegality, the charter of the United Nations rules out "the threat or use of force" between states except in response to armed attack. We violated the charter of the United Nations.

Article 15 of the charter of the Organization of American States (OAS) rules out intervention "directly or indirectly, *for any reason whatever*, in the internal or external affairs of any other states" (italics added). We violated Article 15 of the charter of the Organization of American States.

Article 17 of the same charter continues: "The territory of a state is inviolable; it may not be the object, *even temporarily*, of military occupation or other measures of force . . . *on any grounds whatever*" (italics added). We violated Article 17 of the charter of the Organization of American States as well.

Secretary of State Shultz tried to put a veneer of legality on the invasion by citing a request for intervention from the Organization of Eastern Caribbean States, a tiny group with a mutual treaty to which the United States is not even a signatory. The wording of the "request," however, originated in Washington and was then offered to the Organization of Eastern Caribbean States by United States emissaries. "The legal justifications," as the *New York Times* commented, "were a sham."

The sharp rebukes from such countries as France, West Germany, and Great Britain, the 11–1 vote in the United Nations Security Council deploring the invasion (ours was the lone negative vote), and the 108–9 vote against the invasion in the United Nations itself give some indication of the degree to which the rest of the world was appalled by what the administration did.

2. *The reasons given for the invasion were unconvincing and dishonest.* We were initially told that the invasion was carried out to ensure the safe evacuation of the hundreds of American medical students on the island. There was no effort by the United States to arrange an evacuation by peaceful means. Moreover, there was no indication that the students were in imminent danger or had requested evacuation. On the day before the invasion the airport at Grenada was open and students could have left had they desired to do so, although the White House told us categorically that the airport was closed.

White House officials also told us they feared "another Iran": that is, the seizing of the students as U.S. hostages by an unfriendly regime. If the administration were to follow this logic consistently, the United States would be forced to invade every country with a government unsympathetic to ours. Indeed, the selective decision to save our citizens only on Grenada suggests a lack of concern for U.S. citizens elsewhere, who must be presumed to be in equally dire straits.

We can only conclude that the students were used as a cover-up for other reasons to invade, and some of the students, after initial personal joy at their "liberation," soon began expressing second thoughts. Well they might.

As though anticipating a cool reception to the humanitarian argument, Mr. Reagan soon escalated his rhetoric, proposing that the seizure of Grenada was crucial to our worldwide struggle to "contain communism," since (as he told us in a nationally televised speech) Russia is the root of the problem in Grenada. This is not a new string in Mr. Reagan's rhetorical bow, since communism exported from Russia is routinely perceived by him as the source of all the world's evils. The argument failed, however, to address the question, "Why Grenada, now, and in this fashion?"

The discovery of a "Cuban presence on the island" appeared to give the President some after-the-fact justification for ordering the invasion, though his admission that U.S. intelligence sources had underestimated that presence indicates that the invasion was not launched on the basis of hard evidence that Grenada had become a Cuban-Soviet launching pad to export terrorism.

The further argument that we invaded at the "request" of nearby islanders and the Grenadans themselves did not fare well in the face of challenges, noted above, to its accuracy and legality.

The public reasons offered for the invasion, in other

words, were insults to the intelligence of the American people. And since the administration refused to level with us, we can only speculate as to what was going on in the President's mind while he was weighing his unilateral and illegal decision.

Since Mr. Reagan does consistently wish to "contain communism," it must have seemed attractive to "contain" a tiny bit of communism in a place where significant opposition was impossible and victory was assured. Here, he must have thought, is "a war we can win"—a sentiment with enormous appeal to a president who just two days earlier had seen his "Lebanon policy" collapse with the death of 241 U.S. Marines, and who very much needed a military victory somewhere else to offset that presidential miscalculation. A number of White House aides noted (not for attribution) that the mood at 1600 Pennsylvania Avenue the week before the invasion was dominated by the administration's need to show the world that it was not a "paper tiger" and the feeling that a victory over Grenada could rehabilitate the image of a macho Uncle Sam.

We may not admire such a scenario, but we could at least have acknowledged its forthrightness, in comparison to the flimsy and hastily constructed justifications actually offered.

Such acts of deception leave us in a deplorable situation; we can no longer trust our leaders to tell us the truth. As unconvincing reasons for the administration's actions multiply, we are left with two disconcerting alternatives: (1) Either our leaders are clear about what is going on, but wish to hide it from us; or (2) they are not clear about what is going on, and cannot hide it from us. Both alternatives are unattractive.

3. *The invasion was subject to a degree of government censorship and news management without precedent in our history.* No reporters were allowed to cover the invasion, nor even to go to Grenada itself until four

days after the event. All the news came from the Pentagon; all the footage on TV was shot *and censored* by the U.S. military.

This may be the most disturbing feature of all, for it threatens the core of any free society—the right to know. The censorship demonstrated not only an explicit disdain for the civilian right to know but an implicit desire to cover up anything that might go wrong. Some things *did* go wrong; three days after the military had bombed a civilian mental hospital, killing at least two dozen inmates, the White House was still telling us there had been "no civilian casualties."

Why did the administration ban the press? Secretary of Defense Weinberger first informed reporters that they had been excluded because of the Defense Department's concern for their personal safety. Such tender solicitude convinced no one, and Mr. Weinberger later admitted that the top military leadership had not wanted the press there and that he had not felt free to challenge their judgment. This admission reveals the extent to which civilian control of the military (a cherished democratic tradition) is being replaced by military control of civilians (an initial tilt toward the national security state).

Press censorship goes against the grain of American history. The military did not ask to have the press excluded from the Normandy invasion, or from the multiple landings on Pacific islands in World War II, or even from riding on the B-29 Superfortress, the *Enola Gay*, when the first atomic bomb was dropped; one cannot imagine Franklin D. Roosevelt or members of his cabinet acceding to such a request. Disdainful of that heritage, however, the Reagan administration said, in effect, "We are arbitrarily putting a cloak of secrecy over what we are going to do. Ordinary citizens are not entitled to have us accountable to them. We remain accountable only to ourselves." To think this way, and even more to act this way, represents a sizable stride toward Orwell's *1984*. Even right-wing columnist William Safire thought the censorship was a bad idea—a considerable tribute to the magnitude of its iniquity.

Censorship is a form of news management. If the only available news comes from the military, the military's version of the news will be the only news we get. If the administration has a propagandistic reason for a certain action, a propagandistic version of the action is all we will get. The administration used the process efficiently. We saw no dead American bodies, no pictures of those dead Grenadan hospital patients, no interviews with our own troops after they were mistakenly strafed by our own planes. We did see pictures of selected students being brought home—those who knelt, upon alighting from military planes, to kiss the Florida soil and told us on national television how wonderful the Marines were.

We were given a part of the story, but only a part, and to create the impression that the part equals the whole, as the administration did with consummate skill, is to tamper with the truth. A friend of mine had a telephone call from Europe the day after the invasion. "Well," the European friend commented, having been exposed to Europe's almost unanimous condemnation of the invasion, "your President certainly calculated badly, didn't he?" It was a voice from another planet. We had learned at home from the censored news releases that the President had calculated magnificently.

4. *The consequences of the invasion for the United States and the rest of the world are disturbing.* Here are a few of them:

> • The administration has surrendered whatever high moral ground it still possessed when it comes to future dealings with the rest of the world. Although the magnitude of the events differs, there is no difference *in principle* between our unilateral and illegal assault on Grenada and the Soviet Union's unilateral and illegal assault on Afghanistan. One could take the formal justifications offered by the two nations for their respective invasions and, by adapting a few words,

make them mutually interchangeable. The administration has lost the privilege of taking moral umbrage at Soviet initiatives made without regard for morality or humanity; it now stands exposed as having a similar lack of regard for other nations' borders or for international charters to which it is a signatory.

• If there is to be any curbing of the administration's impulse to shoot from the hip and ask questions afterward, it may have to come from the pressure of worldwide opinion. Domestic safeguards did not work, and to this day the administration cites the Grenada invasion as one of its shining hours. Great Britain, France, West Germany, the United Nations, and other groups must see to it that criticism of the Grenada invasion continues, so that the United States will not dare to repeat the action elsewhere. While we cannot be sure it will make any difference to those already steeled against criticism, a chorus of worldwide reminders of the wrongness of what we did must continue.

• The reasons advanced for the Grenada invasion can be tailored to fit any other invasion the administration wishes to justify. An invasion of Nicaragua would make equal "sense," a concern we will examine in the next chapter. A similar rationale would allow us to create a permanent military presence in El Salvador or Honduras (where we already have thousands of troops), or even Costa Rica, as a launching pad for an invasion. Any scenario in Nicaragua or elsewhere is now possible, and we can be sure that contingency plans for most of them already exist in the files of the State Department.

• The administration's "gunboat diplomacy" (as many have openly called it since Grenada) raises grave questions about trusting such an administration with decision-making power over when to fire the nuclear weapons now located in Western Europe. Given the Grenada precedent, can any European ally trust the administration not to act unilaterally and illegally again?

The issue is idolatry

What is the theological issue at stake in the Grenada episode? Once again the issue is idolatry, the worship of a false god. The state is the false god, and the state is worshiped. Caesar demands exemption from criticism. There is no sin the Bible condemns more consistently.

To say that "the state is worshiped" is to say that its right to do whatever it pleases—such as invade another country—is not to be challenged. If other nations challenge that right, they are ignored. (Asked for his reaction to the news that the United Nations had condemned the U.S. action in Grenada, the President responded, "That didn't upset my breakfast one bit.") If citizens appear likely to challenge that right, information is withheld from them. If members of Congress challenge that right, they are told to rally behind the President and that if they fail to do so, they will be accused of being "soft on communism." If members of the press challenge that right, they are denied permission to see what is actually going on. If churches challenge that right, they are told that religion and politics don't mix. If those within the inner White House circle challenge that right . . . but those within the inner circle do *not* challenge that right; they have been screened ahead of time to preclude such possibilities.

There is another aspect to idolatry, which goes like this: If you wish to make your own position invulnerable to criticism, concoct a devil theory to account for evil. This too the administration possesses. There is a devil out there—an "evil empire," as the President described it to a group of Christian evangelicals in Texas. It is the Soviet Union. Any action on our part—such as the invasion of another country—is justified when it has as its purpose the containment of communism, which is a synonym for the Soviet Union.

Like most Americans, I have little love for the way the Soviet Union behaves, either toward those within its

boundaries or toward those outside. But I cannot believe
in a world of absolute goodness (our side) and absolute
evil (the Russians). I cannot accept a worldview in which
it is wrong to invade a country if the Russians do it but
all right to invade a country if the United States does it.
The ability to discriminate between "Stalinism," "communism," "socialism," and political positions to the left
of William F. Buckley, Jr., is certainly one of the keys
to human survival. To lump them all together in one
indiscriminate mass of evil, as the President does, is a
recipe for more Grenadas and more U.S. support of
fascist dictators all over the world, so long as they are
"anticommunist."

Grenada, then, is a clear example of what happens
when Caesar tries to play God and becomes a false god.
There could be few clearer examples of that to which we
must say No.

One way to say No to past folly is to work to see that
such folly is not repeated in the future. We do not need
"another Grenada," any more than we need "another
Vietnam." That we might have "another Grenada" in
Nicaragua makes it important to look next in Nicaragua's
direction.

Items for Reflection

---

1. What are some of the reasons why Caesar—any
Caesar—is tempted to play God and demand uncritical
allegiance? Relate such reasons to the United States' action in Grenada. Can Caesar ever settle for anything less
than the national security state?

2. Under what conditions might press censorship by a
government be justified? Were those conditions met in
the case of the Grenada invasion?

3. Is the United States entitled to engage in actions
on the international scene (because it is a democracy)

that other nations are not entitled to engage in (because they are "leftist")?

4. Is there any reason why a sovereign nation like the United States should hold itself accountable to other nations or permit other nations to influence the way it carries out its domestic or foreign policy?

5. If idolatry is the theological issue at stake in the Grenada invasion, how does one challenge the false gods that are at the center of one's own national life? Does saying Yes to the God of justice mean saying No to false gods *even within one's own nation*, when they seem to be challenging the supremacy of the God of justice?

6

Nicaragua
and the Double Standard:
When Truth Is a Casualty

There is a gestation period of about nine months between the completion of a manuscript and its availability
in book form. Somewhere during that interval the author
loses control; it is suddenly too late to make changes in
the text, either to update it or to correct errors. On no
topic, perhaps, is it riskier to write within such con-
straints than Nicaragua, so rapidly do new events take
place; what one writes in September may be hopelessly
dated by June.

Nevertheless, the risk must be embraced, for the policy of the present administration toward Nicaragua provides the most contemporary example of why our saying
Yes to the God of justice may force us to say No to
Caesar. And without possessing a crystal ball, I fear
that the gloomy scenario sketched in this chapter will
turn out not to have been gloomy enough. For all the
evidence suggests that the present administration long
ago made a decision that the government of Nicaragua
must be destroyed and that it is willing to do whatever
is necessary, including military intervention, to ensure
that destruction. If it can pay other soldiers to do the
job, that is preferable; but if not, the administration is
prepared (as Secretary of State Shultz has said publicly)
to send in American troops. Why we have the right to
impose our will on another sovereign power is not

explained; our determination to do so is simply demonstrated by each succeeding action. Another Vietman? Yes. Another example of Caesar trying to play God? Yes. Another example of truth becoming a casualty? Yes.

By way of background

There have already been many casualties in Nicaragua besides truth, and by the time this appears in print there will have been many more. The worst casualties, of course, have been sustained by the Nicaraguan people themselves. Forty-two years under the ruthless dictatorship of the Somoza family (kept in power by successive United States Republican and Democratic administrations) took a terrible toll: imprisonments, torture, disappearances, firing squads, informers; not to mention economic deprivation, as the Somoza family brazenly took land and money from the already poor. (When the Somozas were finally toppled, their landholdings had become so extensive that if their land had been distributed to the peasants, each one would have received more than five acres.)

When this situation finally became intolerable, there was a popular uprising in which the Somozas were defeated and fled (with all their millions) to Miami and elsewhere. Before leaving, however, they completed the devastation of their country by killing thousands of those in rebellion and systematically blowing up all the factories, office buildings, and other construction they could.

Consequently, when the Sandinistas (a coalition of many groups—left, right, and center) assumed power in July 1979, the cities and countryside they inherited were devastated by civil war, the population was decimated, the people were war-weary, and the country was desperately poor, without significant resources for rebuilding.

Largely because of the enmity of the United States,

things have not only remained that way but gotten
worse. By *military* means (giving military supplies to
antigovernment guerrilla groups that engage in border
raids on civilians, and building up a massive military
presence in Central America); by *economic* means (imposing a trade embargo that makes it illegal for U.S.
business interests to trade with Nicaragua); by *political*
means (seeking to line up other nations against Nicaragua); by *illegal* means (mining Nicaraguan harbors in violation of international law and issuing manuals
urging the murder of Nicaraguan political leaders); and
by every other means at its disposal, our administration
has sought to crush Nicaragua (make it "say uncle" is the
phrase Mr. Reagan uses)—a country that wishes to build
its future free from the control of any outside nation,
whether the USA or the USSR. In the process of doing
all of this, the administration has created another casualty in addition to the Nicaraguan peasants. That casualty is truth.

Why has the administration done this? It has decided
that Nicaragua is a Russian satellite, that it represents
the tentacles of Moscow reaching onto "our continent"
(as Defense Secretary Weinberger likes to call it), and
that all means that will unite the American people
around Nicaragua's destruction are appropriate.

The administration's claim that this poverty-stricken
nation's three million inhabitants are plotting to destroy
the United States is not shared by most of the rest of
the world, so the United States is increasingly isolated
in its anti-Nicaraguan posture. The isolation only suc-
ceeds, however, in making the administration's rhetoric
more strident and its assertions of the Nicaraguan threat
more excessive.

What we need is an understanding of the ways in
which our leaders manipulate the truth to support their
claims. We do not have the moral privilege of remaining
silent when truth is a casualty. In seeking to sort out

truth from falsehood, however, we are not called upon to whitewash everything that has happened in Nicaragua since the final overthrow of the Somozas on July 19, 1979. For us to see everything in Nicaragua as good, the way our administration sees everything in Nicaragua as evil, would simply be to create a mirror image of falsehood. The Nicaraguan government and the Nicaraguan people are no more exempt from errors of judgment or of policy than any other government or people, and there have been unfortunate instances of press censorship, political arrests, peremptory acts against individuals, discriminatory moves against minorities (such as the Mesquito Indians), and so on. Such policies and activities should be criticized and their correction called for; it is particularly important for people generally supportive of the Nicaraguan experiment to maintain critical rather than uncritical support. Otherwise they participate in a new form of idolatry themselves.

With that point clear, we can examine ways in which the government's treatment of Nicaragua needs to be challenged.

Five ways to make truth a casualty (with extensive help from the United States Government)

1. *The double standard that confuses specks and logs.* We are warned in the Sermon on the Mount that we should first take the log out of our own eye before seeking to remove a speck from someone else's eye (Matt. 7:3–5). That is always good advice, but the admonition can be pressed even further in relation to our government's treatment of Nicaragua. For while it never occurs to the administration that it might have a log in its own eye, it is continually engaging in a microscopic examination of Nicaragua's presumed sins in order to magnify specks into logs, while ignoring or minimizing the massively visible sins of other nations (usually na-

tions we support) so that their logs shrink to the size of specks. And whenever this happens, truth becomes a casualty.

• When guerrilla fighters in El Salvador were threatening to defeat the repressive Salvadoran government that the United States supported, Secretary of State Shultz urged more military aid for the Salvadoran government because the Salvadoran guerrillas were trying to "shoot their way into power." Simultaneously, he made the reverse case concerning Nicaragua, urging more military aid for the Nicaraguan guerrillas, conveniently ignoring the fact that they too were trying to "shoot their way into power." In the first case, shooting one's way into power was immoral; in the second, it was acceptable. A double standard.

• When South Africa was experiencing widespread rioting and murder and governmental repression in the summer of 1985 because of its morally repugnant doctrine of apartheid, the United States continued a policy of "constructive engagement" and "quiet diplomacy," even though it was clear that the South African government would never yield on the principle of separation of the races. Simultaneously, the White House announced that it was "impossible" to work diplomatically with the government of Nicaragua, although it was not experiencing rioting and murder as the result of morally repugnant doctrines. (If there was any "governmental repression," it was minuscule in comparison to that of South Africa, and the Nicaraguan government was already in the midst of effecting widespread reforms in its earlier acknowledged errors in dealing with the Indians.) A double standard.

• While supporting the terrorist regime of Marcos in the Philippines (whom both Secretary of State Shultz and Vice-President Bush have commended for significant progress in the achievement of human rights) and the terrorist regime of Pinochet in Chile (which the United States helped to bring to power and whose repressive measures it has supported for over a decade), the administration works for the outright overthrow—not reform—of the government of Nicaragua, whose record on human rights is infinitely superior to that of either the Philippines or Chile. A double standard.

2. *The undocumented statement that turns out to be false.* One reason the administration can employ the double standard so effectively is that it bases its assessment of Nicaragua on undocumented statements that turn out, upon examination, to be false. A refinement of this position, also widely employed by the administration, is to make so-called "documented statements" in which the documentation itself turns out to be false.

• When Alexander Haig was Secretary of State, a white paper was issued by the State Department charging that Nicaragua was a conduit for arms being shipped from Russia via Cuba to rebel groups in El Salvador. The documentation was so unconvincing that the paper, sent to European heads of states to enlist anti-Nicaragua support, engendered no support whatever.

• When the Sandinistas held their promised elections in 1984, Mr. Reagan denounced them as a "sham" even before they were held. Teams of independent observers, however, from dozens of countries (employing the old-fashioned method of making assessments after, rather than before, the events they were evaluating), were almost unanimous in supporting the high degree of fairness and honesty in the electoral procedures. Even the leader of the most conservative party in Nicaragua asserted that the elections had involved no fraud. Yet U.S. administration officials continue to purvey the undocumented before-the-fact assessment.

• The State Department leaked a report that a shipment going from Russia to Nicaragua contained MIG warplanes, and the report was used for a full week to arouse anti-Nicaragua sentiment in the United States. When the shipment arrived and was unloaded, it contained no MIGs.

• The administration announced that the Nicaraguan government had just started building a new airport with runways designed to accommodate Russian bombers. A former U.S. military official pointed out that work on the airport had begun under the Somoza regime and had nothing to do with Russian bombers.

• On a level that reveals the embarrassing ignorance of U.S. government officials and their lack of genuine reasons to link Nicaragua and Russia, Vice-President Bush announced in early 1985 that a new Nicaraguan stamp had a picture of Karl Marx on it—clear proof of Moscow-Managua connections. What Mr. Bush did not know was that the same series of stamps included *(a)* a portrait of George Washington and *(b)* a reproduction of the signing of the United States Declaration of Independence.

3. *The self-fulfilling prophecy that puts small truths at the service of big lies.* One of the most effective ways of making a casualty of truth is to create a self-fulfilling prophecy, in which a small fact that by itself may be true is presented in such a way that its truth communicates a lie. The administration's self-fulfilling prophecy is usually some variant of the theme, "Nicaragua is developing closer and closer ties with Russia, just as we predicted." What is not stated is that to the degree that this is true, it is often due to the actions of the United States.

• It is true that Daniel Ortega, the president of Nicaragua, went to Moscow in the spring of 1985 (as well as to a number of other countries), where he arranged for shipments of farm machinery, grain, and other agricultural necessities—a clear indication, according to our administration, of increasing dependence on Russia. But it is also true that several months earlier Nicaragua had applied to the Inter-American Development Bank for a $58,000,000 loan to purchase the same kind of agricultural equipment and that Secretary of State Shultz (in an almost unprecedented move) had intervened to urge that the loan be denied. Unable to get help from the bank, Mr. Ortega had little recourse but to turn elsewhere. A self-fulfilling prophecy was created by Mr. Shultz's action.

• It is true that Nicaragua has been engaging in a military buildup, increasing the size of its army and purchasing more arms and equipment, which the administration claims it is doing for the purpose of invading neighboring countries. But it is also true that the United States has been engaging in massive military maneuvers off both Nicaragua's coasts (the so-called Big Pine operations), basing many U.S. troops in Honduras and building huge airstrips there, mining Nicaraguan harbors and bombing Nicaraguan oil supplies, and providing vast amounts of military aid and advice to the *contras,* the rebel troops in Honduras and Costa Rica who are seeking the military overthrow of the Nicaraguan government. In the face of these multiple military challenges to its survival, Nicaragua has had no choice but to increase its defense capability, fearing an attack either by United States troops (for which Grenada provides clear precedent) or by mercenaries openly trained and paid for by the United States. A self-fulfilling prophecy is continually strengthened by U.S.-initiated military actions.

• It is true that Nicaragua has been seeking to increase its trade with eastern bloc nations and with Russia, a fact the administration cites to prove that Nicaragua is increasingly under communist influence. But it is also true that President Reagan initiated a trade embargo against Nicaragua that makes it illegal for U.S. corporations to do business with Nicaragua. Unable to trade with the United States, Nicaragua has no recourse but to trade elsewhere—eastern bloc, Russia, wherever. A self-fulfilling prophecy is created by Mr. Reagan's action. (This prophecy, however, may not be as successfully fulfilled as the other ones, since, to Mr. Reagan's surprise and disappointment, no other nations of any consequence have joined in supporting the embargo. On the contrary, viewing the embargo as unwise if not downright silly, many of our own allies have been increasing their trade with Nicaragua to help make up the gap created by U.S. withdrawal.)

4. *The extravagant rhetoric that sees reality in reverse.* The above devices for making a casualty of truth are strengthened when highly placed officials make statements about Nicaragua that are patently false and repeat them frequently enough so that listeners will begin to assume they must be true. (In dictatorships, this technique is called "The Big Lie.") An unintended

result of this device is that the truth can often be discovered by believing the opposite of what the government official says.

• Mr. Reagan consistently refers to the Nicaraguan government as "terrorist" and the country as a "terrorist
jungle." At the same time he refers to the U.S.-backed
contras, who are trying to destroy the government, as "freedom fighters," often likening them to our own "founding
fathers." The truth of the matter is the reverse: if we are
going to employ rhetoric about "terrorists" at all, it is the
U.S.-backed *contras* on whom the title must be bestowed.
There are hundreds of documented cases, compiled by international teams of observers, of the terrorist activities of the
contras, who sweep over the border from Honduras, murder
civilians, rape women, kidnap children, burn crops, destroy
granaries and warehouses, and attack hospitals and child
care centers. To the degree that there are "terrorists" in
Nicaragua, they are almost exclusively terrorists who have
been funded, supported, and trained by the United States.
If the *contras* truly represent our "founding fathers," they
represent a chapter in our own history of which we can only
be ashamed.

• In a speech on worldwide terrorism, Mr. Reagan cited
Nicaragua as one of five nations in a "confederation" of terrorist nations "now engaged in acts of war against the government and the people of the United States." The President
gave not a shred of evidence to support this charge in the
case of Nicaragua. However, while his extravagant rhetoric
makes no descriptive sense as he states it, its reversal is
painfully true. For there is evidence galore, as we have
already seen and will see again in a few paragraphs, that
"the United States is engaging in overt acts of war against
Nicaragua." Once again, truth is a casualty.

5. *The demonic assertion that we alone are not subject to the truth.* The worst casualty to truth comes
after it has been so manipulated that the manipulators
can redefine it to suit their own ends. This represents the ultimate attempt of Caesar to usurp the role of

God. There is a clear example of this in our relations with Nicaragua.

• The United States has engaged in many illegal activities in Nicaragua, such as blowing up oil refineries near the coast, but none has been more blatant than its mining of Nicaraguan harbors in an effort to scare off ships trading with Nicaragua. Such action is illegal under international law, and our government knows it. After unsuccessful attempts to deny the mining by blaming it on "independent" *contra* forces, the United States had to acknowledge responsibility for the action.

That is bad enough, but what is even worse is that when the Nicaraguan government quite rightly responded by appealing to the World Court for a judgment against the United States in this matter, the Reagan administration decided that rather than subject itself to international law or acknowledge the constraint of truth, it would refuse to do either. So in an act of disdain for truth, the administration responded by announcing that for the next two years it would refuse to recognize the jurisdiction of the World Court in any matters pertaining to Central America. The truth would be that *whatever the United States wished to do it would do*, and that it would not consider itself answerable to anyone else. Truth would be determined by no body of world opinion, no World Court, only at the whim of what was convenient for the administration.

The fact that the administration's heavy-handed decision to thumb its nose at international law has engendered so little domestic protest is itself a symptom of how deeply the sickness has invaded our entire society. Our nation marches along a terrain marked by the earlier presence of the Pharaohs and the Caesars—all of whom likewise set themselves up as definers of truth—and there is no outcry.

The necessity of saying No

If there is a single point at which, in commitment to the God of justice, we must say No to the false god oi

national idolatry, it is surely in relation to the matter
now under discussion. For without that No, truth is not
only a casualty but a casualty that may have little hope
of recovery. When lies become official policy, truth has
a hard time making a comeback. How can we say No
effectively?

First, we can insist on a distinction between our country and our government. We must make our own the
statement of Albert Camus, "I should like to love my
country and still love justice." Let it be clear: it is because we say Yes to what *our country* ought to represent
("liberty and justice for all"), that we must say No to
what *our government* has come to represent ("truth . . .
on the scaffold, wrong . . . on the throne"). When a
government traduces the ideals of a country, it is *an act
of loyalty* to oppose the government. Let us never con-
cede that because people have been elected to public
office they are exempt from challenge and critique; on
the contrary, they are more than ever subject to challenge and critique, because they now speak and act not
just for themselves but for all of us; what they say and
do on our behalf is something for which we can be held
morally accountable.

We can make a *second* distinction, this time between
the executive and legislative branches of government.
In the case of Nicaragua, it has been the executive
branch, the White House, that has initiated most of the
policies designed to destroy the Nicaraguan government.
For a long time it was the legislative branch, the Congress, that ensured whatever restraint remained in our
policy. But in May 1985, the backbone of Congress
melted, which left the way open for the White House to
engage in an increasingly unfettered policy of destruction.

For citizens who find this policy appalling, the only
way to change it through the political process is by re-
newed pressure on Congress to reinstitute its earlier
restrictions. Pressure must also be exerted on the administration to give genuine rather than lip-service sup-

port to what is called the Contadora process, the attempt by a group of Central American nations to develop policies upon which the Central Americans themselves can agree.

Unless our nation forgoes its disastrous decision to use military means to solve political problems in Central America, there will be an escalating double tragedy: the tragedy of the further killing of Nicaragua's peasants by terrorists acting in our name and with our blessing, and the tragedy of our great nation increasingly locked into the consequences of an ideological obsession that bears almost no relation to reality.

A *third* way of saying No to the government is saying Yes to forces trying to create an alternative policy. One ongoing group, the Emergency Response Network, alarmed by the escalating U.S. military presence in Central America, sponsored acts of civil disobedience across the nation in the spring of 1985 to register to our government, to Nicaraguans, and to the world that there were U.S. citizens who opposed the policies of their government. The Network seeks to evolve new strategies of protest for new situations, and those who are willing to commit civil disobedience, or give legal support to those who do, can contact it through local Quaker meetings.

Another group offering an alternative is Witness for Peace, which has sent hundreds of United States citizens to Nicaragua to embody a nonviolent presence of solidarity with Nicaraguans. Often staying in the dangerous northern border areas, members of Witness for Peace say, in effect, "We are willing to share with you the physical danger of the *contra* raids, to tell you and the world that there are U.S. citizens who want to support you with hands of helping rather than destroy you with arms of death." Such visitations also expose more and more U.S. citizens to the realities of Nicaraguan life in contrast to the fantasies of administration rhetoric.

Other groups are seeking to challenge President Reagan's trade embargo, the effect of which will only be to make a poor nation poorer. Nicaragua, for example, needs farm equipment, much of it formerly purchased in the United States, and various church groups, such as Clergy and Laity Concerned, are seeking to express solidarity with the Nicaraguan farmers either by arranging for farm equipment to be shipped from other countries or by taking it themselves and directly defying the presidential edict. The latter is a serious act of civil disobedience, with potentially heavy penalties, and it is a tribute to those making such plans that they place a higher priority on alleviating human misery than on obeying what they believe to be a cruel and unjust directive by their head of state.

It is sad that people must be pushed to such measures in an attempt to be faithful to the God of justice. But only in this way will the modern Caesars realize that they are playing a losing game, even by their standards, and begin to respond to the best instincts of the people of the United States rather than imposing their own worst instincts on the people of Nicaragua.

A personal postscript

This has been a partisan chapter, and some readers may feel that it is so biased as to be unfair. But I am unable to apologize for either its tone or its substance. For in any discussion of Nicaragua more is at stake than ideas, which can be discussed in genteel fashion. Human lives are at stake, and they can never be discussed in genteel fashion. They can only be discussed with passion. If someone loses a life because my voice or my actions were too genteel, I am accountable. I do not want Nicaraguans to be killed any longer, and I do not want my country to be part of the process that continues to kill them.

The reason for my concern can be focused in a single image: the children in the child care center of the Nicaraguan border town of Ocotal.

When one of the teachers comes into a room banging a pan, the children immediately stop whatever they are doing, get down on the floor, and slither on their tummies into a central room, heads down, mouths open. They are playing a wonderful game of pretending to be fish.

What the children do not know is that the game is deadly serious and is designed to save their lives next time the U.S.-backed *contras* conduct a terrorist assault on the village, where (as a member of the U.S. Embassy told us) it is perfectly justifiable to attack child care centers, since that is where the "ideologues" of the future are being trained. By keeping their heads down, the children may avoid drawing sniper fire, by keeping their mouths open they may save their eardrums from the concussion of artillery, and by going to the central room with its reinforced roof they may survive a bomb attack.

The *contras* would not be threatening that child care center in Ocotal if they were not receiving U.S. military aid. They might not know all the niceties of guerrilla warfare (such as attacking child care centers and kidnapping children) if some of their leaders had not been subjected to the wisdom of U.S. military advisers. They would not have the food and trucks and supplies to maintain their armies without what is euphemistically called "humanitarian aid" provided by Congress.

The ongoing military aid the United States gives to the *contras* is not creating a modern counterpart of our "founding fathers," Mr. Reagan's rhetoric to the contrary notwithstanding. It is only enhancing the likelihood that future generations will remember this period of our history as the time when we were the butchers of the children of the poor.

Items for Reflection

1. If "shooting one's way into power" is immoral, how do we justify our own American Revolution?

2. If you were a head of state in Europe or Latin America, what reasons would you give for supporting, or not supporting, the U.S. policy of forcing the Nicaraguan government to "say uncle"?

3. What measures are there for countering the various manipulations of truth? Are there times when a government is justified in employing falsehood to implement policies it considers crucial?

4. Are nonviolent protests or civil disobedience ever justified except in "emergency" situations? Does Nicaragua present an emergency situation?

5. The church in Nicaragua is divided on the question of support of the present government, with some of the bishops strongly opposing, and many of the priests, sisters, and laypeople strongly supporting. Several highly placed government officials are priests. (For interviews with them on reasons for their working so directly with the political forces despite orders from Rome not to do so, see Teofilo Cabestrero, *Ministers of God, Ministers of the People: Testimonies of Faith from Nicaragua;* Orbis Books, 1983.) How do Christians make decisions when the church leadership is divided?

7

South Africa:
Beauty in the Midst
of Ugliness

Whatever the outward situation in South Africa when these words are read, we can be sure that the inner situation will not be tranquil. For South Africa is in the midst of an irreversible journey which, whether it takes years or generations, will continue until the last vestiges of apartheid (the so-called "separate development" of the races) have been eliminated and blacks can, for the first time, control their own lives. The destination may take a long time to reach, but reached it will be, whatever the timetable. This is because increasing numbers of South African blacks and whites are recognizing, as we saw in chapter 1, that to say Yes to Jesus Christ means to say No to apartheid.

People of goodwill, both inside and outside South Africa, disagree on the most feasible—that is, the least costly—way to get rid of apartheid. When it seems as though violent revolution is the only realistic course for blacks to follow, we have the amazing spectacle of Rev. Desmond Tutu, the black Anglican bishop of Johannesburg, counseling the need for radical change, all right, but counseling nonviolence as its only realistic vehicle, and fearlessly entering a crowd intent on burning an alleged informer to death in order to save his life—and, quite incidentally, demonstrating the correlation in his own life of word and deed. (When Rev. Jerry Falwell,

a self-designated expert on South Africa after a five-day
visit, dismissed Desmond Tutu as a "phony," he removed
himself permanently from the ranks of those whose future judgments need to be taken seriously.)

What is most important for those of us who are not
South Africans is to listen as carefully as we can to the
voices of the victims, those who have paid, and will
continue to pay, a heavy price for their convictions. Just
as there are occasional blacks who pander to the white
South African government and are publicly endorsed by
that government (and by Mr. Falwell) as though they
spoke for the victims, so there are occasional whites who
have broken with the white supremicist line and say No
to the government at a personal cost inconceivable to the
rest of us in our privileged safety. The words that shape
the future of South Africa will finally come from blacks,
as these few courageous whites know. And as blacks
increasingly gain their own spokespersons and leaders,
their cause will be increasingly invincible.

In apparent disregard of this fact, I have chosen to
comment on South Africa through reflections on a recent
book by Alan Paton, a white South African, called *Ah,
But Your Land Is Beautiful* (Charles Scribner's Sons,
1981). Paton played a central part in sensitizing the consciences of white South Africans in opposition to apartheid, and as leadership passes now to blacks like Bishop
Tutu, Allan Boesak, and others, it is fitting to honor this
brave man who, since his first novel, *Cry, the Beloved
Country*, has played a central part in sensitizing the
consciences of whites elsewhere as well. His book not
only shows us some of the subtleties of South Africa
we need to understand but also leaves us uncomfort-
ably aware of how much more the situation in South
Africa is like our own situation than we usually care to
acknowledge.

What seems far away is actually close at hand.

One finishes *Ah, But Your Land Is Beautiful* and
longs to cry out to the author, "Ah, but your book is

beautiful, Mr. Paton." And then one reflects: A beautiful book about ugliness, how can that be? How does its author continue to find, within the sordid, those gleams of the sublime which sometimes redeem, for moments at least, the ugliness that always threatens to destroy them? How does he keep alive the sounds of hope when one by one they seem to be drowned out by the stronger sounds of orchestrated evil?

Beauty and ugliness within the human heart

I think Paton is saved in large part by his characters— characters who are not only creations of his heart and soul (which tells us something about his heart and soul) but are also people he has really known, sometimes identified by their true names and sometimes renamed or made composite. He shows us something stronger than evil in the lovely Indian woman Prem Bodasingh, who is both gentle and tenacious; in the irrepressible Emmanuel Nene, who knows he will be hurt but embraces his hurt for the sake of others; in Laura de Kock, occupation housewife, who deals with the police on her terms, not theirs; in Trevor Huddleston, Helen Joseph, even crusty old Archbishop Clayton; and in many more unnamed— such as the little old woman who challenges the great Dr. Fischer after he has said that for the sake of retaining their own culture blacks should not ever worship in white churches, and she, in a meeting where the secret police are present, responds that whites deny the use of their church buildings to black people "not because of any desire to help them cherish their racial identity, but because of the hardness and coldness of our hearts."

But Paton does not entice us to the sentimental hope that a few small acts of courage will be sufficient to upset a ruthlessly efficient system determined to keep the races separate. He helps us to learn, along with almost all the liberals in his book (whether white, black, colored, or Indian), that "to sally forth with goodwill does not necessarily get you anywhere in politics."

Such realism saves Paton from those sins of lesser novelists, generalizing and stereotyping. While there is a Christian humanism that underlies his story, he does not use it to manipulate, nor does he offer religion as a panacea that will set things right. For alongside pastors like Isaiah Buti of the Holy Church of Zion, in whose ears the cries of the shattered ones are never stilled, he shows us Dominee Krog and Dominee van Rooyen, who will not conduct a white man's funeral as long as blacks are in the sanctuary, and Dominee Vos, who will not bury a white man who has touched the breasts of a black woman, and so not only offended against the law but shamed his race. And when Paton depicts the security police in Capetown who destroy the life and marriage of poor Mr. Lodewyk Prinsloo because it is discovered that one of his parents was colored instead of white, he depicts as well the white magistrate in Soetrivier who sentences four white youths to a year in jail for throwing a black man off a bridge because he refused to give way when there was not room to give way. Many of Paton's blacks are courageous, but he acknowledges that being black does not automatically confer courage; in a world where white men betray, so too can black men betray. A black leader, Robert Maguza, can say to three black policemen who are informing on members of their own race, "A prostitute sold her body and Christ forgave her, but you sell your souls, and whether you will ever be forgiven, I do not know." What Mr. Maguza does know is that his own words will not be forgiven.

It must have been a temptation to Alan Paton to portray those with evil ideas as living evil lives through and through, the better to legitimate the rightness of his cause. But he lets their humanity emerge enough so that we are caught off guard and cannot have our villains neat. Even Gabriel van Onselen—the epitome of the proper functionary who believes in everything for which his government stands—is not carved in granite. He not only has his moments of self-doubt, he even has his moments of compassion. When his rival, Jan Woltemade Fischer, is destroyed, Van Onselen does not gloat. Quite unexpectedly, he is touched by the tragedy to Fischer's mother and befriends her, far beyond any need or sense of duty. But when deeds of befriending threaten his career, the doors of compassion close, and doctrine triumphs over decency.

In Van Onselen, Paton gives us a clue to the tragedy of evil rule anywhere, which is not that such regimes are ordered by unambiguously evil men but that they are ordered by men who could have been good and were captivated by evil. And when they try to own the evil by calling it good, it means that the evil owns them.

The plight of the well-meaning

It is the subtleties of a government that break people, Paton reminds us, the subtleties that become less subtle as the human targets of their campaigns are manipulated along a spectrum from annoyance to anger to fear to terror. For whites to accept the institution of apartheid is to feel guilty but to benefit from it. But for whites to challenge the institution of apartheid is to start down a road that leads inevitably from the subtleties to the terror. Paton shows us Robert Mansfield, a decent, courageous white who resigns from his job to work for the Liberal Party. And we watch the calculating escalation of harassments by persons unknown—from the sand in the auto engine, to the neutralizing of the brake fluid, to the bullets through the living room window that almost kill his guest, to the bombing that is designed to kill his daughter.

What shall he do? Stay and continue to place the lives of guests and children in ongoing jeopardy? Or leave and begin life again somewhere else? And if he leaves, how will he cope with his guilt toward those who stay despite the danger? Who can truly blame him for leaving? And who can truly urge him to stay? It is, as he tells a friend, "a cleft stick," the plight of well-meaning people caught up in the consequences of trying to follow conscience.

In the case of Hugh Mainwaring—of the respectable Durban Mainwarings—the government interrogators are also subtle at first, but smoothly move in to disclose their purpose: We know everything about you; we know where you were that night; we know you slept in the same house as an Indian girl; we also know you slept in separate bedrooms, so this time no charge is brought against you under the Immorality Act; but we know all that you do, and we will destroy you, family connections or not, if you persist in challenging the policies of your government.

Paton not only describes the plight of white liberals. The blacks, as he shows so poignantly, get the worst of it, for they have no power at all. And yet even so, as he also shows us, they *do* have power—power that frightens those who govern them. There is a rare courage that sometimes enables blacks to taunt the security police rather than being reduced to jelly in their presence, that prompts them to organize to fight for homes the government wants to take away from them, even the courage to join with whites in the struggle. And that last takes rare courage, for where in their history is there anything to persuade blacks that whites, any whites, can be trusted? That there is nevertheless trust, both given and received, may be the greatest gift of grace in all of South Africa.

The word "grace" has been used. What are we to make of Prem Bodasingh, the young Indian woman, one of the most grace-filled, graceful women in contemporary fiction? If at any point Paton has succumbed to the temptation to create a human being without flaw, it is in the creating of lovely Prem Bodasingh. And yet she remains believable, clear in her vision of what she must do to fight the fierce laws that deny dignity to her people;

single-minded in her conviction that to run away and marry (since, being in love with a white man, she could only marry by running away) would make her despicable in her own sight and his; committed "to the death" in her struggle—a commitment she is almost called upon to honor.

The redemptive power of a deed

There is a scene in the Holy Church of Zion that has a fearsome beauty, during which powerful forces of evil are, for a moment, redeemed by a gentleness of equal power. The scene is a series of surprises. Paton has prepared us for the fact that Judge Olivier is a man of character, standing againt his fellow jurists on issues where principle is involved. But even he cannot fully prepare us for the fact that when a black pastor asks the judge if he will come to the black church on Maundy Thursday and wash the feet of Martha Fortuin, the black woman who helped to raise the judge's children, the judge replies, "She has washed the feet of all my children. Why should I hesitate to wash her feet?" Could we have anticipated that the great Judge Olivier, remembering how Martha Fortuin had kissed the feet of his children, would be moved, after washing her feet, to kiss them in return, far beyond the call of instruction or expectation? Paton prepares us for the fact that when news of Judge Olivier's action is reported in the press, it will cost him the Chief Judgeship that should have been his. But we could not have known, when the black pastor calls on the judge to ask forgiveness for involving him in an act that destroys him professionally, that Judge Olivier would respond, "Taking part in your service on Thursday is to me more important than the chief-justiceship. Think no more about it."

There is something deep here, a faith that puts persons above custom, however deeply embedded. For it is custom, deeply embedded, that white men do not go to black services; nor do they wash the feet of black women; nor, especially, do they kiss the feet of black women. It is not done.

But it was done.

There were tears in the eyes of most within the church. And there were tears in the eyes of many who later read of the incident that was never meant to be a part of public knowledge. As Trina de Lange wrote the judge, "There is so much grief in our land that when one suddenly encounters joy it sets one to weeping." Yes, cry the beloved country; and it sets one to weeping elsewhere too. Mr. Paton has been given the holy power to elicit tears. May he always use it sparingly, but use it well, for it is likewise the avenue to joy. There is a land, he reminds us (alluding to the book of Revelation), where tears will have been wiped away from every eye and there will be no more sorrow and no more pain. But in the land of South Africa, that time has not yet come. There can be little joy without tears as well.

To his credit, Paton does not claim too much for such an episode. He includes right after it a leftist editorial denouncing Judge Olivier's act as white condescension at its worst—irrelevant, if not harmful, in the face of the reality that Martha Fortuin's wages are probably three or four percent of the judge's wages and that "such gross inequalities are not removed by any amount of washing or kissing." Yes, that is a truth to ponder.

And there is another truth to ponder, that the day after Maundy Thursday is always Good Friday, when goodness was crucified, also amid tears, with little room for joy. And no one can claim that in South Africa, or any land where injustice is rampant, there has yet come an Easter when crucified goodness is raised up. Or is the real truth that raised-up goodness is prefigured in the Maundy Thursday service in the Holy Church of Zion, a church they want to rename the Church of the Washing of the Feet?

The far away is close at hand

Ah, But Your Land Is Beautiful is painted on a wider canvas than Paton has ever used before. There is a whole nation of characters this time, with cloven feet and hearts of stone, although sometimes the feet are shod with the gospel of peace and the hearts are full of deep compassion. Sometimes both of those contradictory impulses are struggling for survival within the same human breast; in blacks, whites, coloreds, Indians, Afrikaners, English-speaking, liberals, Nationalists, dominees, priests, pastors; in Nhlapo, who has it made as well as a black can make it within the laws of the land and is loath to give it up just short of retirement on an adequate pension; and in Nene, who has it made as well as a black can make it within the laws of the land and gives it up anyway and finds security through the not-so-simple act of letting go of security. It is the spectrum of a whole generation—a generation in which all sought the glory of moving "into the Golden Age" but also shared the tragedy that by the Golden Age they meant contradictory things. And as long as people mean contradictory things by it, there will be no Golden Age.

One whose name is never mentioned beyond the title page is also part of the story, a moving spirit behind the forces for good described beyond the title page, and that is the author. Paton has been a faulty chronicler in leaving himself out of his story, and someday another chronicler must repair an omission founded on modesty.

But even with the insertion, we have not yet seen the full width of the canvas. For just as Paton writes about himself without writing about himself, so he also writes about the rest of us without writing about the rest of us.

If we could believe that he was writing only about South Africa, we could close his book conscience-free and thank God that we are not like all the rest. But he leaves us unable to do so. For his microcosm of South African injustice reflects the macrocosm of the world's injustice. Like South Africans, we have our own racism, more subtle and therefore at least as dangerous as theirs, and when we are honest, as Paton forces us to be, we must acknowledge that there is some of it in every human heàrt. Like South Africans, we make our own compromises with the truth, doing it "for the sake of our children," or in response to counsels of prudence, or out of concern for our pension plans. Like South Africans, we have our public selves, rational, consistent, and firm (counterparts of Dr. Fischer); and our inner selves, irrational, erratic, and weak (counterparts of Dr. Fischer). And also, like South Africans, we sometimes see nobility of spirit displayed in those from whom we least expect it.

The baseness and the beauty that in mixed proportions is the stuff of every human being is what we have in common with Paton's characters and his world. His land is our land as well. We are, globally, counterparts of the handful of whites who still rule South Africa. But we know, and they know, that it will not remain so forever, and that no Golden Age will be built on such a premise as apartheid. And if we do not know it, or do not choose to acknowledge that we know it, his book is the reminder that it will not remain so forever, and that as he told us many years ago through Msimangu, in *Cry, the Beloved Country*, our own greatest fear must be that when we have turned to loving, they will have turned to hating.

Beauty with potential to redeem

Why do people say, "Ah, but your land is beautiful"? Alan Paton's visitors in South Africa tell him that it is because of its mountains, its vineyards, its hills and valleys—lovely beyond any singing of it, as he himself affirmed on the first page of his first novel. But he reminds us, beyond all such impressions, that there is a greater loveliness, a greater beauty, than that bestowed by nature. It is the beauty bestowed by *human* nature, a beauty dazzlingly apparent to all who have eyes to see, when blacks walk twenty miles a day to work in protest against an unjust rise in the bus rates, risking arrest by doing so. And he asks us, in perhaps the most important question we need to have addressed to us, "What is more beautiful than those who walk to their work, along the hard pavements of Louis Botha Avenue, day after day, week after week, in sickness and in health, because they think their cause is just?"

The question shows us how it is possible to have beauty in the midst of ugliness and how a book about ugliness can be beautiful. For the beauty of the land is not finally a beauty in the fields where the titahoya sings, but a beauty in the hearts of men and women who, standing in the midst of the ugliness of injustice, refuse to accept its power over them and, for themselves and for their children and for all the rest of us, daily seek to redeem the ugliness and show how—this is goodness indeed—it can still be transformed into a thing of beauty.

Items for Reflection

---

1. In light of the increasingly explosive situation in South Africa (see the front page of any newspaper or the top item on any news telecast), is it still possible to find "beauty" in people walking silently to work in political marches? What other measures are called for?

2. Should U.S. firms continue their business connections in South Africa? Will their presence raise the level of black opportunity sufficiently to offset the implicit support their American presence gives to apartheid?

3. In light of the viciousness of apartheid, is it a sufficient U.S. response to continue a policy of "constructive engagement" when this enables the South African government to believe that the United States will continue to support it even in the presence of apartheid?

4. If apartheid creates a *status confessionis* for the

churches in South Africa (see chapter 1), what should be the policy of their sister churches in other parts of the world toward *(a)* the South African churches, *(b)* apartheid, and *(c)* similar instances of injustice in their own societies?

5. If we recognize, as Alan Paton does, the ambiguity and divided loyalties in the human heart, will that make it more difficult to oppose evil, since we will find some of it in all of us?

6. Is it still possible to believe in beauty in human nature, when evil, ugliness, and oppression result from perversions of human nature?

7. Is it really fair to draw parallels between the South African situation and our own? Aren't the expressions of racism so different in our two societies that different estimates and strategies are called for? Or is the whole question a white middle-class cop-out?

8. *Note:* Appearing too late for comment in this volume is an extraordinary report, issued in the fall of 1985 by a great variety of South African church signatories, called *The Kairos Document.* It calls upon Christians to disavow "state theology" that supports apartheid, "church theology" that is essentially addressed to white South Africans and cannot get to the root of the problems, and to opt instead for a costly "prophetic theology" that works for radical change and a new government. The document may well become a counterpart in our day of the Barmen Declaration. The statement forms an important basis for further reflection on issues raised throughout this book. Copies are available for $1.00 from the Stony Point Conference Center, Crickettown Road, Stony Point, NY 10980.

8

Poland: Caring in the Midst of Betrayal

Alan Paton shows us that even in the worst of circumstances a few people, in saying Yes to their deepest convictions, can say No to the counter-convictions of their society and simultaneously create a beauty that is believable in the midst of ugliness, even when the evidence overwhelmingly proclaims the folly of believing.

Sometimes the odds are even more overwhelming, and a single individual or a single family must, in saying Yes to a despised minority, say No to a majority that has unlimited power to destroy.

In a town in Poland, the generalities of the preceding paragraphs were miraculously transformed into human specifics. Let us call the town Z. Before World War II, Z was a town of craftsmen and farmers, with about fifteen hundred Jewish families. The Jews had their own cultural life centered around their rabbis in the various small prayer houses, along with one main synagogue.

When the Nazis arrived, the Jews were forced to live in a ghetto, from which they were systematically deported. So when the Nazis left, the town of Z had become small town of craftsmen and farmers, with no Jewish families, no ghetto, and no synagogue. According to plan, all the Jews had been rounded up and sent to the death camp of Treblinka, and the main synagogue had become a social club for Gentiles.

The "final solution" had worked in the town of Z. There were no Jews left.

Or so the Nazis thought. But their count was off. Off by four. For a Jewish mother with two sons and a daughter survived eighteen months of Nazi occupation in the town of Z, hidden by a Catholic family in the garret and basement of their home.

I heard the tale, and then relived the tale, through the eyes and ears of Eli Zborowski, one of the sons who survived, and who went back to the town of Z thirty-five years later, to visit the family that had saved his life. It was designed to be a joyous reunion. It *was* a joyous reunion, but only after a scary disruption. This is his story, now become two stories: the earlier story of the grandeur and the terror of being a Jew, but also the contemporary story of the grandeur and the terror of being a Jew.

Eli's father, a merchant, contracted with a builder to construct a house for his family. One of the builder's employ ies was a young Catholic bricklayer. Every noon, the young bricklayer remembered, Eli's father would come by during the lunch hour with a bottle of vodka, and the group of them would eat and drink and converse together. To the Jewish merchant, the workers were not just workers doing a job for him, they were persons with whom he liked to associate. And so they all became fast friends.

But they did not all live happily ever after. When the Germans came, the Jewish merchant had to jump out of the second-floor window of the synagogue into the river. Two miles upstream he was apprehended by fellow Poles. Rather than hiding him, they shot him. After all, he was a Jew That was the last Eli Zborowski ever heard about his father.

Before his death, the father had made a heavy request of the young Catholic bricklayer and his family: in the event of trouble, would they be willing to shelter a Jewish family? In all the other occupied countries of

Europe, such an action meant arrest or deportation. In Poland, however, it meant death.

The bricklayer, not surprisingly, asked for time to talk it over with his family. Two days later he gave his answer; it was affirmative. And that is why, some months later, Eli's mother and her three children were spirited into a garret one dark night. And since garrets were already notorious as places to hide Jews, the bricklayer also constructed a bunker in the basement of the house, fronted by a false brick wall that fit into place so cleverly that it could not be detected. (Being a bricklayer had unexpected dividends.) The bunker was very small, not large enough to stand in, but large enough for four people to hide in for a few hours when word had gone out that the Germans were conducting a sweep of the neighborhood, on the lookout for hidden Jews. In times of such immediate danger, the Zborowskis would be shunted to the cellar; when the immediate danger was past, they would return to the attic, where there was only the "normal" danger of being apprehended and shot or transported, gassed, and cremated.

The Catholic family had an eight-year-old daughter who was not party to the conspiracy for a very simple reason: eight-year-olds do not hold up very well under torture. The daughter sensed that *some*thing was strange but not *what* thing was strange. Hearing noises in the garret, she asked what they were and was told that a cat had been installed up there to patrol the mice. "It must be a very big cat," she replied, content to let the matter drop.

Eighteen months passed this way, with about ten emergency transfers to the basement bunker. Food was passed up each day, and wastes were passed down each night. And every hour of every day and every night, a sentence of death hung over the entire household.

The imminence of death was telegraphed on the night the eighteen months came to an abrupt end. A friend came over to have a drink with the Catholic family; the father made a splendid brand of gooseberry wine. After several glasses, the friend said in an unguarded moment, "You are hiding Jews." The moment he left, a tense assessment took place. Had the comment been a threat of disclosure, or a hint that word was getting around? Was it a taunt or a warning? No time to investigate. Mother and children left the next night for another place of hiding. Six days later the Nazis broke into the house, demanding not "Jews" but "Zborowskis." Someone had informed.

But thanks to the chance warning of a friend (if it was a warning), four Jewish lives were saved, and because there was not enough evidence to bring charges against the Catholic family, three Catholic lives were saved as well. Years before, Eli later reflected, his father had done a mitzvah, a good deed, in having lunch daily with his work crew. If it had done the father no direct good, it had nevertheless saved the lives of his wife and children. If the Poles who shot Eli's father were craven before the Nazis, other Poles refused to surrender their humanity or the humanity of others.

So, thirty-five years later, Eli Zborowski, one of the sons, was returning to the town of Z. The mother and daughter of the Catholic family were still alive, and there was to be a reunion. A television director from NBC was along, to film the story of the return. So was Eli's wife, Diana. Diana had lost her entire family in World War II and was understandably apprehensive about returning to Poland, let alone to the town of Z, but this was an occasion designed to offer an alternative to ongoing fears.

And with them all were three of us—Protestants, as it happened—to share in the joy. A truly ecumenical situation: a Jew, whose life was saved by Catholics, returning to his hometown with Protestants. Why did he ask us? Since Christians saved his life, Eli told us very simply, he wanted Christians to share in his celebration of that fact.

Tony, the television director and a real pro, recorded Eli's entrance into the town of Z, though it took longer than anticipated, because of the unexpected noise of the traffic and a particularly uncooperative cow, who insisted on trying to steal the scene during a succession of retakes.

The cow successfully circumvented, Eli showed us the house in which he was born, and then the house in which he grew up. The camera recorded all, before a crowd of youngsters, both excited and appreciative, who followed us from street to street; how often, after all, had television cameras been to the town of Z? There was one adult in the crowd who was as excited as the children but definitely less appreciative. We soon learned why he had left abruptly. For when we arrived at the next filming site, the police were waiting for us.

"What are you doing here?" they asked Tony, not kindly. "Why are you filming the houses of former Jews?" And then, "You must come to the police station for interrogation."

Tony tried to pass it off. "Later," he responded. "The light is fading."

No concession was forthcoming. "Right now," was the response, and off they went into a labyrinth of side streets, the television director in tow. He played it cool, assuring us that a few explanations would clear every-thing up. We should wait for him.

When twenty minutes had passed and he had not reappeared, Eli Zborowski, not lacking in guts, decided to go to the police station himself to investigate. And so Eli too disappeared into the labyrinth of side streets. We stayed in the car with his wife, who was, understandably, increasingly apprehensive. "I want to get out of this town," she said. "This is just like thirty-five years ago. The police take people off for 'questioning' and they never return. As soon as Eli and Tony are back we must leave."

But Eli and Tony didn't come back, and so finally we

too made our way toward the police station. At the station, as we learned later, the television director had continued to play it cool. He, in fact, had no trouble establishing his identity. "Yes, we know who you are," the police chief said, "we've seen you on TV. But what are you doing here with these Jews."

The question was not inflected. It cannot appropriately be rendered in italics. It was matter-of-fact. That is what made it so devastating. Diana Zborowski was right; it was like thirty-five years ago.

Anti-Semitism is alive and well in the town of Z. . . .

The civilian official who had lodged the complaint saw Eli walk into the police station. He turned to the television director and asked, "What are you doing to us, bringing these Jews back here?"

Eli started to protest: "I was born here. I have a passport, a visa. I have come to see friends." He was abruptly cut off by the official.

"You are not wanted here."

Alive and well, indeed, in the town of Z. . . .

Phone calls had already been placed to Warsaw. An answer was being awaited. Eli, adrenaline flowing, pursued his questions. He had been born here, he had a passport, a visa, he had come back to see friends, what were the charges against them? The police chief did not like the word "charges." Patiently he explained the linguistic facts of life to Eli: they had not been "arrested," so there were no "charges " They were only being "detained," until "clarification" was obtained from Warsaw. Eli pressed his point: "There are no charges? Then that means we can leave?"

No. "You must wait until the phone call is returned."

Finally, after another half hour had elapsed, the phone call was returned, queries having gone to "the highest authorities." Apparently Warsaw could identify no crime being committed. The "detainees" could leave. Having proved that they were not guilty, their innocence could again be assumed.

A tiny incident. A tiny, ugly incident that elicited apprehension on my part, even fear. It elicited anger on Eli's part. Somewhat against my Protestant temperament, I must report that anger was a better response. For Eli Zborowski consistently refused to be intimidated, as we discovered the moment we all got back into the car. Shouldn't we leave town after this kind of treatment? Indeed no. Now more than ever we should go on with the filming.

We went on with the filming. We filmed the synagogue-now-a-social-club, from which Eli's father had jumped. And then—grace-filled climax—we went to the home where the eighteen months of befriending had taken place thirty-five years before. It more than redeemed the tiny, ugly incident. The wife, though ill and very feeble, was waiting for us, as was the eight-year-old daughter, now going on forty-four. She was a large, plain-looking woman, but whenever she engaged another person in conversation, her face became radiant.

We had two hours of healing radiance.

Although the home was small and simple, this was clearly an Occasion. There was special tea, there were homemade Polish doughnuts, and there was a bottle of gooseberry wine which the daughter produced, saying (the only time she broke down, so that the radiance was sprinkled with tears), "We have saved this bottle for a special time. It is wine my father made immediately after the Germans left, thirty-five years ago." We drank to the father, to the reunion, to the health of the ill mother, and to the future happiness of the hearty daughter.

Their joy in seeing Eli, his joy in seeing them, their immediate acceptance of his wife into the family, told us more powerfully than words can ever do that kindness, and decency, and willingness to risk on behalf of another are still central to the human story, despite police interrogations, and that a single expression of those qualities thirty-five years earlier bears fruit that can be harvested forever.

Even the joy of that reunited table, however, was not
without its shadows. A woman from the other side of
town, obviously a party functionary, burst in without
knocking. She had heard about a "commotion," and she
wanted, curtly, to know just who these strangers were
who had come to town. And the television director, who
had gone out to take background shots during the meal
in the house, returned to say that he had been asked
three times on the streets, "Why do you bring Jews back
to Z?" Three times.

Alive and well, indeed. . . .

But when the curt woman had left, and the television
director had returned, the old mother, breast heaving
from the emotion of the entire experience, told us not to
worry, and explained that some people in town still hated
them, thirty-five years later, for having harbored Jews.

"I do not understand," she said lucidly. "We are all
Catholics here. Why should they object to what we did,
when our Lord told us to help those in need? When I ask
them, they have no answer. So do not worry."

We asked her how, in the face of this, she had borne
up under years of hostility from people who had once
been her friends. Her eyes moved to a simple holy picture on the wall, of the Virgin suckling the child Jesus.
"She feeds us all," was her fully adequate response.

We went down to the basement and saw the bunker,
and saw how the fake brick wall worked, and how small
the bunker was, and remarked on how claustrophobic a
place it must have been. Well, yes, Eli gently reminded
us, but not as claustrophobic as a gas chamber.

As we came up the tiny stairs and prepared to leave,
the old woman, having gathered in the course of the
translated conversation that two of us were Christian
ministers, asked for a "blessing" and for prayers for her
health.

And then there was a beautiful moment. For her, I
prayed a very "Catholic prayer," using imagery she
could understand, invoking the intercession of the saints

and the healing power of Jesus, the Great Physician. The two of us then laid our hands upon the venerable head and blessed her. And those Catholic words, on the lips of Protestants, were translated for her into Polish by a Jew.

The Kingdom of God is also alive and well in the town of Z.

Items for Reflection

---

1. The record of Christian support for Jews during the Hitler era is very bad, and the members of the family in this story were a distinct minority. What convictions make it possible to stand against the majority and say Yes to unpopular positions at great cost?

2. What common features are there between saying No to the United States government's position on Nicaragua, the South African government's position on apartheid, and the Nazi government's position on the Jews? What sort of Yes is needed to make such costly No's possible?

3. Is it morally permissible to lie to governmental authorities when asked such a question as, "Are you hiding Jews?" Is there a danger that answering deceptively in this situation will encourage deception in other situations?

4. How much can we count on tiny movements to redeem ugly situations? (Recall Judge Olivier's washing the feet of Martha Fortuin in the preceding chapter as well as the action of the single family in the town of Z.) Is it sentimental, or realistic, to bank on them for wider changes in the long run?

5. Are there comparable situations in the United States where the survival of specific human beings depends on our willingness to say No to certain governmental policies? (If nothing comes to mind, proceed immediately to chapter 9.)

9

Sanctuary:
Can We Still Say Yes to God
and Yes to the Law of the Land?

Had we lived in the town of Z described in the preceding chapter, we would surely want to have been numbered among the handful who sheltered Jews and saved them from death rather than among those who turned Jews over to the authorities or turned their backs on Jews and made their capture and death inevitable. We may even feel twinges of envy that people back then had such clear-cut decisions confronting them, whereas our choices are murky and ambiguous.

Or are they?

It is the contention of this chapter that the choice that people confronted in the town of Z (shelter these Jews or they will be killed) is the same choice we are facing in the United States today (shelter these Central American political refugees or they will be killed). Saying Yes to the God of justice means saying No to the perpetrators of injustice, whether their victims are Jews or Salvadorans. How has it come about that such choices should face us as well?

El Salvador: a land of terror

Since the beginning of the 1980s, over fifty thousand civilians have been murdered in El Salvador. There are "governments" in El Salvador, run either by the latest

victor in a military coup or by civilians who are beholden
to the military for their political and physical survival.
The government itself is directly responsible for many of
the murders, and "death squads," usually either sponsored by the government or acting with its tacit approval, are responsible for the rest. The murders appear
haphazard and random, until one discovers the single
consistent feature: anyone who opposes, or is presumed
to oppose, or knows people who oppose, the policies of
the government sooner or later ends up dead, usually
after prolonged torture.

Despite this parlous reality, our State Department
and the White House routinely announce every six
months to Congress that El Salvador is making "significant progress" in establishing human rights. This gives
Congress the opportunity to vote more money to the
Salvadoran government . . . to buy more guns . . . to kill
more civilians. . . .

An exercise in imagination in the world of reality

Imagine that you are a Salvadoran and that you oppose
this way of running a country and have the temerity not
only to say so but to work for change. If you have friends
or relatives who have done so, you already know their
fate: they "disappear" without a trace; or their bodies
turn up in ditches, terribly mutilated; or, if they are
women, they are gang-raped before being shot, or their
unborn children are ripped out of their wombs before an
assassin's bullet mercifully ends their lives. And you
know that that sort of routine treatment of "dissidents"
is in store for you once they catch up with you, which
might well be tonight. As your friends and associates
begin to receive that treatment simply because they are
known to be your friends and associates, and their deaths
give you the message that you had better shut up, you
realize that it is your politics that have rendered their
survival and yours marginal at best. Unless you are

lucky, somewhere along the way you have already been arrested and subjected to torture.

So one night you slip away, and after weeks of surreptitious flight you arrive in the United States, with its long history of welcoming the stranger, and you ask for asylum as a political refugee until it is safe to go back to El Salvador. You know that according to the laws of the United Nations and the Geneva Convention you are entitled to such protection, and you also know that the United States has its own law, the Refugee Act of 1980, that makes similar provision for your safety within its borders, if you have a "well-founded fear of persecution" in your own country of sufficient magnitude that you dare not return.

So you present yourself to the immigration authorities, asking for refugee status in the United States, since in El Salvador your life is not worth a plugged peso.

The United States immigration authorities tell you (and approximately 97 percent of the people like you) that they do not believe you are a political refugee at all; they inform you that you have come to the United States not because your life is threatened back home but because you are in search of big bucks. You are an "economic," not a "political," refugee, they tell you, and they are quite hard-nosed about it. The fact that you have marks of physical torture on your body is not sufficient evidence to them that the Salvadoran government dislikes your politics. And since the "death squads" have not cooperated by providing you with a notarized affidavit that you are next on their hit list, the immigration authorities are unimpressed by your plea for political asylum. Petition denied, next case.

And so the United States Government puts you (and approximately 97 percent of the people like you) on an airplane and deports you back to the San Salvador airport, where the "death squads" have compiled an im pressive record of tracking United States' deportees once they leave the airport and seeing to it that the do not survive long enough to cause trouble for this government of El Salvador that the State Department tells us is making such "significant progress" in establishing human rights. As Archbishop Rivera y Damas (no flaming liberal) reports, "It is a sad fact that Salvadorans have returned to this country only to meet their death a few days later." It is small consolation to you that the archbishop has anticipated the nature of your homecoming.

If you had had the good fortune to be a refugee from an Eastern European country or from any other "dictatorship of the left"—a Russian ice skater, perhaps—your story would have been very different. In that case, the granting of your refugee status would have been almost as automatic as the denial of your refugee status was when you had the misfortune to be fleeing from a "dictatorship of the right"—a dictatorship that the United States Government supports with money, arms, and military advice.

Your predicament: While there are laws guaranteeing you the right of asylum from political persecution, they are enforced with such grotesque unevenness by the immigration authorities and the State Department that you hardly stand a chance.

The Sanctuary movement:
caring in the midst of betrayal

It was out of such circumstances that the Sanctuary movement emerged in American churches and synagogues in the early 1980s to ensure that political refugees from El Salvador (and Guatemala, where conditions are just as bad) were provided with the protection the law is supposed to guarantee.

The notion of "sanctuary," of caring for the stranger, is as old as the Jewish tradition: "When strangers sojourn in your land," the book of Leviticus counsels, "you shall not do them wrong. The strangers who sojourn with you shall be to you as the natives among you, and you shall love them as yourself; for you were strangers in the land of Egypt: I am the Lord your God" (Lev. 19:33–34, adapted). By the fourth century of the Christian era, and during the Middle Ages, Christian churches were frequently places of refuge and safety where people in danger were protected from unjust actions of the lawless or even vindictive upholders of the law. During the Hitler years, individuals sometimes provided places of safety for Jews, as we saw in the last chapter, and one town in France, Le Chambon, became a kind of sanctuary area for Jews, as townspeople by the hundreds conspired to cheat Hitler of his full quota of Jews for the death camps. (A moving account of these collective acts of courage and mercy by the stubborn Huguenot community is contained in Philip P. Hallie's *Lest Innocent Blood Be Shed;* Harper & Row, 1979.) Although the *legal* assurance of sanctuary in a building has long since vanished, during the Vietnam War many churches provided *symbolic* sanctuary for American men who felt they could not fight in what they perceived to be an immoral war and were facing serious legal penalties as a result.

As political refugees from El Salvador and Guatemala in the early 1980s found their requests for political asylum almost routinely turned down by the immigration authorities, they began appealing to the churches for help, and it was the tradition of sanctuary that the churches invoked in their response. So when pastors and church members close to the U.S.-Mexican border began to provide church facilities, it was in order to give the refugees assurance that they would not be peremptorily deported while seeking to regularize their status through the courts and gain possession of the rights to which the Refugee Act of 1980 entitled them. In addition to providing living space, food, clothing, and medical services, the churches provided legal counsel as well, since violations of the civil rights of refugees by the Immigration Service were egregious. *Their intention was not to "break the* law" but to see that the existing law was enforced. Once the legal situation had been clarified, they assumed, the refugees could move out of the church buildings and live reasonably normal lives in the United States until the political climate back home had changed and it was safe to return.

But there was a snag. The immigration officials persisted in denying political refugee status to Salvadorans and Guatemalans.

What were the churches to do? Should they suddenly abandon the refugees, who would be picked up by immigration officials and deported to likely torture and death? The proposal was unthinkable. Churches must continue to provide "sanctuary," work for the enforcement of the Refugee Act of 1980, and press for new legislation that would protect the status of the more recent refugees from El Salvador and Guatemala. In addition, they must continue to give sanctuary to the refugees who continued to pour over the border, since the "death squads" did not declare a moratorium on the killings while U.S. immigration officials got their act together. As Rev. John Fife, a pastor under indictment for his work in the Sanctuary movement, put it, "We will continue to assert the church's right to administer sanctuary to helpless people whose lives hang in the balance every day. We cannot abandon our help to Central American refugees without abandoning our religion, our faith."

As a result, the Sanctuary movement has entered a collision course, not so much with the "law" as with the government's selectively unequal enforcement of the law and the consequent danger in which this places thousands of Salvadorans and Guatemalans.

The government's response: betrayal in the midst of caring

At the time of this writing, immigration officials are still loath to enter church buildings and arrest refugees

who, in the government's eyes, are there illegally. Bad
PR. But the government is increasingly willing to indict
church workers who are giving help to refugees, particularly if they are transporting them from one place to
another, this being, in the government's eyes, a clearly
illegal act. And they are more than willing to arrest the
refugees who are in process of being transported and
have the legal misfortune to be beneficiaries of church
concern. At the time of this writing, twelve pastors,
priests, sisters, and lay workers have been indicted in
Arizona, and many more have been cited as "unindicted
co-conspirators" who may be called to testify in court
against their colleagues. Some of the trials have already
been held and stiff convictions handed down. But most
of the cases will be in the courts for years, and the issues
they raise will remain precedent-setting ones, as long as
the tension between saying Yes and saying No remains
important.

Those in the Sanctuary movement who have been
charged with breaking the law usually offer two central
points in defense of their actions.

First, *it is the United States Government, not the
Sanctuary movement, that is breaking the law.* There is
a clear mandate as we have already seen, in both the
Refugee Act of 1980 and the corresponding provisions of
the United Nations and the Geneva Convention (to which
the United States is legally bound), to provide protection
for political refugees coming from places such as El Salvador and Guatemala. Sanctuary workers are trying to
see that the government enforces its own legislation.
Once the issues are a matter of public record, beyond the
exclusive purview of the immigration hearing boards,
the indictees hope that the discriminatory criteria im-
posed in the past will become apparent and that individuals heretofore denied political asylum will be granted it.

This response is a testing of the question stated in the
title of the chapter: Is it possible to say Yes to the God
of justice (which means standing in solidarity with the

refugees) *and* Yes to the law of the land (which is designed to further, rather than impede, justice)? It would be a decision worthy of wide celebration were the final legal disposition of these cases to be that it *is* possible simultaneously to say Yes to God and Yes to the law of the land. In that case, to borrow from Albert Camus once more, we could love our country and still love justice.

To be sure, any such results would be an embarrassment to the State Department (to which the Immigration Service, an agency of the Justice Department, reports) and to the entire administration, for if the courts uphold a finding of widespread murder for political reasons in countries whose governments we support, that will make us complicit in those murders and make a change of policy mandatory. But as between the embarrassment of government officials and the saving of innocent lives, the choice should be an easy one.

Suppose, however, that this first argument is not convincing to the courts (as may well turn out to be the case before this book is published). What then?

Second, if the courts decide that it is illegal to aid refugees seeking political asylum, then many participants in the Sanctuary movement are prepared to continue to say Yes to the God of justice, even if it means saying No to the law of the land (or, at least, the current interpretation of the law of the land). Here is a clear case, they argue, where *rendering allegiance to God precludes rendering certain things to Caesar* (such as Caesar's right to deport refugees to almost certain death), and where contemporary Christians have to say, with the earliest Christians, "We must obey God rather than men" (Acts 5:29) and, with Martin Luther, "Here we stand, we can do no other. God help us. Amen."

What is at issue is not the desire of some far-out church folk to act illegally in order to "score points" against the Reagan administration. (Richard John Neuhaus, an opponent of sanctuary, trivializes the discussion by claiming that this is the principal concern of the

Sanctuary movement.) What is at stake, on the contrary, is the acknowledgment by "regular" church folk that they must act morally, whatever that may subsequently mean about breaking the law. During World War II, Christians did not refuse to shelter Jews because to do so would have meant acting illegally; they gave refuge to Jews because to have failed to do so would have meant acting immorally. We can establish a clear moral principle here: *To save a human life is sufficient reason to break a law.* As long as we can save lives without breaking the law, well and good. But if lives are at stake and the law stands in the way, it is the law that must be sacrificed, not the lives. This would be true in relation to sanctuary even if it could be shown that some of the presumed political refugees are in fact here only to seek better jobs, as the Immigration Service insists. For as Rabbi Wolf Kelman pointed out after the Rabbinic Assembly (representing more than twelve hundred Conservative rabbis around the world) had passed a resolution in support of sanctuary, "If there is a reasonable doubt on matters of life and death, the doubt must be resolved in favor of life."

We have not yet heard the worst. An important part of the story of the Sanctuary movement has not yet been mentioned: the account of governmental infiltration into the Sanctuary churches by means of paid informers and spies in order to gather material for the indictments. It is important enough to need another chapter.

Items for Reflection

---

1. Is the analogy between helping Jews in Germany and helping Central American political refugees in the United States a valid one? If so, what does this suggest about the responsibility of the churches in our society?

2. Are there legitimate reasons why the United States

should refuse to honor national and international laws that guarantee political refugees the right of asylum?

3. Does the contention of sanctuary advocates that the government rather than the churches is breaking the law seem cogent?

4. When all legal means of enforcing a good law or changing a bad law have been exhausted, is it appropriate for concerned citizens to engage in nonviolent civil disobedience in the name of conscience?

5. Sanctuary churches have asked other churches to "declare sanctuary" in order to enlarge the number of places where the rights of refugees are respected. What arguments could be mounted pro and con if your church considered declaring itself a sanctuary church?

10

Paid Informers,
Deception, and Lies:
Another Test Case
in Saying Yes and Saying No

In 1975 I attended the fifth world assembly of the World Council of Churches in Nairobi, Kenya. I have a friend from an Eastern bloc country with whom I try to get caught up on such occasions. We exchange information about our families and compare how our respective churches are dealing with problems of pastoral care and social justice. At Nairobi, we got together for a noon meal, starting out in an isolated part of the dining room. As the tables around us filled up, my friend's voice got lower and lower. Before he spoke he would look around to see who had sat down nearby, who was passing the table, who was simply lingering in the neighborhood.

I realized that my friend was keeping a close eye out for an informer, someone who might hear him say something questionable and report it back home.

He had been conditioned not to trust.

Two years earlier, during a visit to South Africa, my wife and I visited a seminary for black South Africans. It took a long time to establish rapport between two white strangers and those black students. I tried to explain that I could understand their reluctance to speak in front of white people, both of whom could be presumed capable of passing information along to the Special Branch, the South African version of our FBI. One of them indicated just how eager the Special Branch was to keep tabs on theological students. "The day before I came here," he reported, "I was visited by a member of the Special Branch. He said they would pay all my seminary expenses if I would report any conversations with students, or any comments by professors, that were critical of the government. I told him 'No.'"

We could feel a change in the room's atmosphere and sense other students thinking, He says he said "No," but maybe he's pulling a double bluff and is actually reporting what he hears, or, Even if *he* said "No," maybe there are other people in the room who said "Yes." Maybe my roommate is one of them. Maybe that comment I made the other day has already been reported.

They had been conditioned not to trust.

On both occasions, my initial reaction was the same: how lucky I am to live in a country where trust of one's government can be presupposed, a country where the government doesn't hire people to infiltrate the churches in order to betray church members. I had always associated such activities with totalitarian governments, the sort of thing that might happen in Eastern Europe or South Africa, or Hitler's Germany, but not in the United States. Eberhard Bethge, a survivor of the Nazi era, made the German comparison at the time of his own visit to South Africa:

> An observer from Germany can hardly fail to be impressed by the striking parallels with the Hitler period.
>
> To begin with, any meeting of Christians assumes as a matter of course that "informers" and police spies will be present. These informers may be people who have been intimidated into such a role or who are paid for doing this work—and these people include non-whites, who are very vulnerable; or they may be people who have been asked very politely to accept this role and who feel it their duty to support government policy in a situation of supposedly grave national danger. (Eberhard Bethge, *Bonhoeffer: Exile and Martyr*, p. 168; Seabury Press, 1975)

Bethge's description of Nazi Germany in the 1930s and South Africa in the 1970s is now a description of the United States of America in the 1980s. For in 1983 our own government began to engage in the same kind of deception against churches in the Sanctuary movement that is practiced in totalitarian regimes, hiring government "informers" to infiltrate the churches, pass as sympathetic participants, and surreptitiously tape-record what turned out finally to be ninety-one different services and meetings in those churches.

So I confess my naïveté. I had really trusted the integrity of my government, much as I might disagree with many of its policies. I had really thought that lying, cheating, and deceiving were beyond the scope of what the United States Government was prepared to do to betray church members. I know better now.

So do members of Sanctuary churches who have been indicted on the basis of evidence secured in this fashion.

It has not previously happened in the United States of America that evidence surreptitiously gathered at church services, Bible study groups, and prayer meetings has been introduced into a court of law for the purpose of convicting church members of crimes. The effects of such action on the life of the church and upon the integrity of a free society cry out to be explored. Let us do so by posing three questions.

1. What does the government's tactic of hiring informers to infiltrate our churches do to the churches and the church members? The evidence of the people who have been victims of this practice is that the most devastating consequence in the life of the churches is *the loss of trust*. A man wearing clerical garb in Nairobi may be an informer; a classmate in a South African seminary may be an informer; a member of the congregation in Phoenix or Tucson or Palo Alto may be an informer. No one can be sure who is acting honestly and who is acting hypocritically. As a result, church members become less open and trusting; they guard their comments; they begin, despite their best intentions, to act less honestly and more hypocritically themselves.

Linked with the loss of trust is *the rise of fear.* Individuals begin to ask themselves: What will happen if I speak in Bible study or at a prayer meeting? Will I be put on a list? Will I lose my security clearance? Will my job be threatened? Having indicted my pastor, is the government about to indict me? If they have infiltrated my church, maybe they have also infiltrated my place of work; maybe that new employee who was asking at lunch what I thought of the Sanctuary movement is also a paid government spy.

Pastors report that parishioners are now less willing to talk with them over the phone, even about personal matters that have nothing to do with sanctuary, fearful that the line is being tapped, the conversation recorded, and that what is meant to be a confidential discussion might emerge in a transcript at a court hearing. Some church members no longer trust even the atmosphere of the pastor's study, assuming that it may have been bugged by a federal agent without the knowledge of the pastor. Visitors at Sunday morning services tend to be greeted warily: are they for real, or are they also government agents with tape recorders strapped to their legs, recording conversations that might later prove useful in challenging the loyalty of a member of the board of deacons? In one church, where a participant in the Wednesday prayer meeting and the Friday morning Bible study turned out to be a government spy, both activities were effectively destroyed; the participants were fearful that someone else might be hired by the government to tape the meetings surreptitiously.

In addition to the questionable governmental morality being exercised in this matter, there is a legal point to be explored. One of the privileges protected by the United States Constitution is "the free exercise of reli-

gion." It can be argued that for the government to engage in infiltrating and surreptitiously tape-recording
activities within the church is itself unconstitutional. Obviously, people cannot engage in the free exercise of
their religious faith in liturgical gatherings, prayer
groups, and Bible study if they suspect that someone is
taping their comments in order to bring a legal suit
against them. Remarks that would be appropriate in a
small group as a means of eliciting reactions take on
awesome proportions when they appear on a court transcript introduced in the course of criminal proceedings.
Remarks addressed to God in prayer assume a different
character when they become remarks addressed to a
jury, read from a transcript by a clever prosecuting
attorney with a gift of inflection. As long as such consequences surround church activities, it is clear that "the
free exercise of religion" is no longer "free," nor is it
likely to be "exercised." And that is the death of "religion."

Unless the court strikes down the admissibility of evidence secured in this fashion, churches that are serious
about an ongoing commitment to Central American refugees will have to entertain the notion of going under-
ground, at least on this issue, so as not to betray the
refugees. This will mean adopting such criteria of survival as the following: Trust nobody, or at least only a
very few; meet clandestinely; assume that the government is out to get you; use code words for your activities;
make sure nobody ever speaks an ill-advised (i.e., an
honest) word at a larger church gathering.

That is an impossible agenda for most Americans to
entertain. For that is to play right into the hands of
government leaders who would like to tighten their hold
on the people and make dissent increasingly expensive.
And that leads to repression. It is not emotional polemics
to make such a comment; it is simply reporting a fact.
The experience of the church throughout its history has
been that repressive regimes don't appear overnight;
they make their way slowly and quietly, chipping away

at the safeguards of a free society, building up fear and distrust, until by the time people realize what is going on it is too late for effective protest or countermeasures. One of the first steps in such a process is to infiltrate those groups by whom the government has most reason to feel threatened in carrying out its policies, and if the policy is to allow no political refugees from Central America, and the Sanctuary movement is at variance with that policy, then the Sanctuary movement must be infiltrated for the purpose of destroying it.

We are at a stage now in which the government has made a clear decision to try to destroy the Sanctuary movement by legal intimidation. We had better advertise this fact and oppose it while we still have the freedom to do so.

2. What is the effect of government infiltration on the infiltrators themselves? We are told—and it is a hard saying—that we are to love our enemies and be concerned for their welfare, even when they are trying to do us in.

What goes on inside the soul of Jesús Cruz, one of the government's paid spies, who, since he is Hispanic, could pose as a supporter of the Sanctuary movement and make his way into the life of a local parish, all the while taping information to secure the indictment of its members? For a sum of money, our government persuaded him to lie, cheat, and dissimulate; to make friends for the explicit purpose of betraying them; to assume the posture of prayer as a means of spying on the participants in prayer meetings; to engage in Bible study not to learn about biblical trust but to practice human mistrust. Jesús Cruz was not only instructed by our government to become an evil person; he was promised that if he was an effectively evil person, our government would reward him.

I know nothing about the personal life of Jesús Cruz and the other paid informers in the Sanctuary cases, but

I do know that the evidence used in the Harrisburg trial of Daniel and Philip Berrigan was gathered by another paid informer, Boyd Douglas, who had a criminal record stretching over fifteen years. One day our government said to Boyd Douglas: We used to punish you for cheating, lying, and betraying people, but that's all past; now we are going to reward you for doing those very same things. Your vices are no longer vices; they are virtues. Spy on your friends; steal their private letters; give us copies; report their conversations; send us regular reports. If you betray them sufficiently, we will reward you handsomely.

What does that do to the infiltrator? Our government's action helps to destroy whatever lingering sense of integrity and honor the infiltrator ever had. This brings us to a related question.

3. What is the effect of infiltration on the initiating agent, the government? The answer is clear and painful: The government—our government, the government we support and to which we pay taxes—becomes a government that honors deception, rewards acts of betrayal, gives bonus points for telling lies, and destroys the meaning of truth. Our government not only says, We intend to punish those who shelter persons whose lives are endangered. Our government also says, We intend to reward those who help us punish such persons, and we license them to cheat, lie, and dissimulate in gathering the information we need.

And although the government may not say it explicitly, the government is acting out a belief that goes: We do not endorse saving people, we endorse (and reward) deceiving people. We do not endorse concern for the friend in a prayer circle; we endorse (and reward) betraying the friend in the prayer circle by pretending to be a friend in order to become an enemy. It is the deceivers, the informers, the hypocrites who are the government's representatives in the American churches.

Such are some of the unspoken but actual value reversals on which government-sponsored infiltration is
based. They indicate the type of activity our government
will reward and the type of activity it will punish. They
thereby indicate a betrayal of what a democratic free
society is meant to be.

So it is not antipatriotic to criticize the tactics our
government has employed to convict church members in
the Sanctuary trials. It becomes the highest form of
loyalty to protest when the government betrays the
country's highest ideals.

Asked if the evidence gained in this fashion was necessary for the government's prosecution of the case, the
district attorney replied, "The case would collapse without it." Any case based on such methods of gathering
evidence deserves to collapse.

Saying Yes and saying No emerge with clarity in the
face of the government's infiltration procedures.

To say Yes to the God who cares for refugees means
a willingness to care for them ourselves, and is a way of
saying No to the false god who insists that we betray
them.

To say Yes to the refugees means to plead their cause,
and is a way of saying No to those who persecute and
prosecute them.

To say Yes to justice for refugees means to act on
their behalf, and is a way of saying No to their intimidation and harassment.

To say Yes to our heritage of concern for outcasts
means to provide shelter for outcasts, and is a way of
saying No to those who seek to deport them.

To say Yes to those who are putting themselves on the
line for refugees means to stand in solidarity with them,
and is a way of saying No to the forces that are indicting
them.

To say Yes to churches that have declared sanctuary
is to join with them by becoming Sanctuary churches

and is a way of saying No to government attempts to
destroy the Sanctuary movement by intimidation and
destroy the refugees by deportation.

Quite simply: To say Yes to the God of justice means
to act justly, and is a way of saying No to Caesar whenever Caesar acts unjustly.

Items for Reflection

---

1. Chapter 4 indicated that the standard operating
procedure in the national security state is a network of
spies and informers to report any words or actions that
seem to challenge the power of the state, and chapter 7
indicates that this is standard operating procedure in
South Africa as well. Are there any differences between
those policies and the policy in the United States of
hiring people to betray each other?

2. Can one truly engage in "the free exercise of religion" if one is unable to act in response to the demands
of the God of justice?

3. The following episode illustrates—more effectively
than further items for reflection could—what happens to
all concerned when the government uses infiltrators and
spies.

Shortly before Christmas 1984, a delegation appeared
at the pastor's study in a Baptist church in Seattle, a
church that had given sanctuary to an entire Central
American family. They introduced themselves as part of
the Sanctuary group in Arizona, members of the church
that had originally befriended the family and made ar-
rangements for it to relocate in the safer environs of the
Northwest. The group had Christmas presents for the
children of the family and had come to deliver them in
person in order to see to it that the children, victims of
so much upheaval in their lives, had a merry Christmas.
Since the family had moved out of the church building
and into the community, would the pastor give the dele-

gation the new address so that the presents could be delivered in person? In a moment of naïveté, as the pastor later described it, he gave them the new address, and the visitors, after expressing warm thanks, left his study to call on the family.

Only they did not deliver Christmas presents to the children. They arrested the family, in the name of the United States government, for being illegal aliens, and the family, children included, spent Christmas in jail.

There is no record that any presents were ever delivered.

Personal Conclusion:
A Letter to My Grandson

This book contains a lot of discouraging analysis and some stiff proposals for action. Its net result could be disheartening rather than energizing. Since I believe that the Christian message is hopeful rather than despairing, I want to end on a note reflecting that conviction: a talk given at an interfaith rally for peace, held at the Palo Alto City Hall Plaza, on Easter 1983.

The text came from the book of Deuteronomy, where God offers a choice: "I have set before you life and death, blessing and curse; therefore choose life, that you *and your descendants* may live" (Deut. 30:19, italics added). Saying Yes to life, God's freely offered "blessing," means saying No to death, our self-inflicted "curse"—not only for our own sakes but for the sake of all who come after us.

Taking a cue from that text, I framed my words in the form of a letter to my grandson.

Dear Colin:

You, in all the strength of your ten months of life, are here today demonstrating on behalf of peace. This is not the first peace rally you have attended. And, the state of the world being what it is, it will not be your last. To your grandparents and to your parents, not to mention many uncles and aunts, you represent one of

the reasons all of us are here, issuing a call for peace.
For we too want to "choose life," not only for ourselves
but for you and all our "descendants" as well. So you
represent our *concern* for peace.

But in addition, Colin Masashi Ehara, you represent
our *hope* for peace as well. The "Colin" side of you
comes from Scotland and England; the "Masashi Ehara"
side of you comes from Japan, and includes native-born
Japanese along with Nisei and Sansei Japanese-Ameri-
cans. During World War II, your two sets of grandparents were technically known as "enemies." In those
years, there could be no contact between the two sides
of your family except on the field of battle. In an ugly
example of racial hatred, white American citizens even
imprisoned Japanese-American citizens behind barbed
wire simply because of their ancestry.

And yet today, people from those two different back-
grounds, your father and mother, not only can speak
and work together, they can love each other. As you
grow up, you will hear some people pray a prayer by
Francis of Assisi, asking that "where there is hatred,
may we sow love." As you grow up, you will hear other
people say, "Oh, but that's impractical, that's utopian,
that's unrealistic. We can't move from hate to love."
And you, Colin Masashi Ehara, will be the living refu-
tation of such cynicism—a reminder that members of
races who were once called "enemies" now dwell together lovingly in the same house. You will be a living
pointer to the hope that those who *today* are called
"enemies" can one day dwell together lovingly on the
same planet.

Those of us here today come from different back-
grounds and traditions and histories. On many things
we disagree—on taxes, abortion, city ordinances, who
we think will win the National League pennant. But on
one matter we are increasingly united: not only must
we have peace, we must change the ways we work for
peace, since our government's policy of building more

and more nuclear weapons is only leading us closer to
the brink of war—a war unlike all other wars, in that
if it ever begins, there will almost certainly be no sur-
vivors. So our different traditions call us to think and
act in new ways.

The Buddhist meditation read this afternoon calls for
peace at every level of our being. The Jewish Scriptures
put before us a choice between death and life, with the
consequent necessity of turning swords into plowshares, which today means turning MX missiles into
day-care centers, tanks into hospitals, submarines into
schools. The Christian Scriptures talk about "a new
heaven and a new earth," in which all the old things
have passed away and there will be no more sorrow, no
more crying, no more pain. What characterizes these
traditions is a belief that there must be *basic changes*,
brand-new directions. Could there be a more radical
shift than the one from death to life, from swords to
plowshares, from an old earth of pain and hatred to a
new earth of sharing and love?

That's what your parents and grandparents, Colin,
would call "a heavy agenda." And to gain strength for
affirming it, we look not only to words from the past
but to deeds as well, and we make the important discovery that we are not alone. The day of this rally,
April 3, is close to the birthday of one of the buddhas,
one of those from the past who taught and lived a life
in which peace was central. Just a few days ago, Jews
celebrated Passover, the time when they were liberated by the creative power of God from the destructive
power of Pharaoh—quite literally a transition from
death to life. Tomorrow is the anniversary of the death
of Martin Luther King, Jr., who acted out in his life
and death the power of commitment to change. Today
Christians celebrate Easter, the time when their leader
(who, like the Jews before him, was under the power
of another Pharaoh called Pontius Pilate) was liberated
by the creative power of God from the destructive

power of that other Pharaoh, who murdered him and then discovered that he hadn't gotten rid of him— another instance of the power of death giving way to the power of life. And just ten days before this rally, many people joined Roman Catholics in celebrating the anniversary of the death of an archbishop from El Salvador, Oscar Romero, who, like the Jews and like Jesus, took a stand against the forces of evil and death in his own land and was killed by the Pharaohs down there. Before his death he had said, "They may kill me, but I will rise in the hearts of the Salvadoran people." And that is what happened, Colin—out of his death has come new life and courage for his people.

Pharaoh could not destroy the Jews, Pilate could not destroy Jesus, the racists could not destroy Martin Luther King, Jr., the junta could not destroy Archbishop Romero. Such realities, Colin, are signs of hope. They tell us we are not alone. Those who have been leaders of our traditions—Gautama, Moses, Jesus—do not disappear from the scene. They remain to energize us, to remind us that no cause for good and decency is ever a lost cause. And so we take heart.

I wish, Colin, that I could stop there, simply welcoming you to the struggle for peace. But there is something else you need to know. The costs are high. We see the ultimate costs in the deaths of those who work for peace. Many people today who demonstrate for peace are arrested and imprisoned. So the road to peace is difficult and sometimes dangerous, and no one should ever lead you to think otherwise. Most of the people here with you today support the need for a nuclear freeze, affirming that as a tiny first step toward peace we must stop making more weapons of destruction. And yet our President calls those of us who feel this way "dangerous"; he says we are "hindrances" to peace; he calls us "irresponsible." He used to say we were being controlled by the Russians, but last week the FBI clearly demonstrated that he was wrong. Take heart, Colin, when one committed to the struggle for peace says an appreciative word for the FBI.

There will continue to be such charges, from the President and others, and if you choose to work for peace in later years, you will find them leveled at you too; you will be called naïve or dangerous—an appeaser, a coward, a traitor. And one of your hardest jobs will be to try to love such people even as they vilify you. Take heart from the fact that here too you will not be alone; that there is an increasing community of those who will side with you and seek with you to break down barriers of misunderstanding and ill will; and that in whatever religious or humanistic tradition you choose to align yourself, there will be resources of courage available.

There is a final thing you need to reflect on as you grow up, Colin. The call for peace is very wide and very deep. Right now, we need to focus special energy on the issue of nuclear weapons, since those are the most immediate threat to our survival. But the issue of peace is more than the issue of nuclear weapons. Any call for peace, while it may begin with concern about the nuclear threat, must move on to include other things as well.

So if they tell you, Colin, "The freeze initiative passed, so now we have peace"—do not believe them, for we will not have peace as long as nuclear weapons are in place and ready to be launched.

If they tell you, "At long last we have gotten rid of nuclear weapons, so now we have peace"—do not believe them, for we will not have peace as long as conventional weapons can still destroy us.

If they tell you, "We have finally gotten rid of conventional weapons, so now we have peace"—do not believe them, for we will not have peace as long as there is hunger and unemployment.

If they tell you, "We have finally gotten rid of hunger and unemployment by having the rich take care of the poor, so now we have peace"—do not believe them, for we will not have peace as long as there are structures that divide rich from poor and make the poor dependent for their survival on the whims of the rich.

If they tell you, "We have gotten rid of the structures that perpetuate inequality, so now we have peace"—do not believe them, for we will not have peace until the outer structures of the society and the inner leanings of the human heart are in accord.

If they tell you, "We have finally brought the inner and the outer into accord, so now we have peace"— you can begin to believe them.

But always hold up before them a final test: Does what has been attained increase or diminish the chance for children to grow up without fear, without hunger, without human diminishment? For the world you live in now, Colin, is a world in which the privileged are the ones with the money, the weapons, the economic and political power. The world we want for you, and for all like you, is not a world in which those are the privileged ones but a world in which the only privileged ones will be the *children*. So you, and millions like you at every rally and in every land, remind us of why we are here today issuing a call for peace, a call to choose life rather than death, so that not only we but our descendants— you and your generation—may live.